# Potty
# Training
# Magic

# Potty Training Magic

## The fun way to go nappy-free fast

Amanda Jenner

**Vermilion**
LONDON

7 9 10 8

Vermilion, an imprint of Ebury Publishing,
20 Vauxhall Bridge Road,
London SW1V 2SA

Vermilion is part of the Penguin Random House group of companies
whose addresses can be found at global.penguinrandomhouse.com

Penguin
Random House
UK

Copyright © Amanda Jenner 2019
Illustrations © Ollie Mann 2019

Amanda Jenner has asserted her right to be identified as the author of this
Work in accordance with the Copyright, Designs and Patents Act 1988

This edition first published in the United Kingdom by Vermilion in 2019

www.penguin.co.uk

A CIP catalogue record for this book is available from the British Library

ISBN 9781785042393

Typeset in 11/16.5 pt Sabon LT Std
by Integra Software Services Pvt. Ltd, Pondicherry

Printed and bound in Great Britain by Clays Ltd, Elcograf S.p.A.

Penguin Random House is committed to a sustainable future for
our business, our readers and our planet. This book is made
from Forest Stewardship Council® certified paper.

# Contents

# Acknowledgements

While writing this book, so many special memories of all the lovely families and little ones I have met over the years came back to me. I feel lucky to have worked with you all to help overcome some tricky milestones, and I am so grateful to you for inviting me into your homes.

I would like to say a big thank you to my editor Sam Jackson at Penguin Random House for believing in me and publishing this book. Thanks also to Leah Feltham for holding my hand throughout. And thank you to Julia Kellaway – the queen of words – for your editing. Not forgetting Leisa Maloney, my agent, for all your support and motivation. Thank you also to Fiona for all your help, patience and enthusiasm – you have been a star.

I would like to say a big thank you to all my special friends who have been there for me. Thank you for the support you have given me for so many years throughout my journey. You know who you are!

Thank you to my mother-in-law Marie Hughes – without you stepping in and helping, it just wouldn't have been possible to write this book. You are one in a million.

I would like to dedicate this book to my three beautiful children – George, Hollie and Olivia – for all the things you have taught me about being a mum. I have loved our journey together so far and feel so blessed to be your mum. I am so proud of all three of you.

A special thank you to my best friend – my husband Darren. You have believed in me every step of the way and have been by my side encouraging everything I do. Thank you for helping make my life complete and giving me the opportunity to be your wife – I am so lucky.

To my angels Nuna and Nuno – I told you I could do it; I just wish you were here to see, but I know you are watching.

# Introduction

Writing this book has long been a huge desire of mine. When I was seven years old my mother left us due to a marriage breakdown, leaving myself, my nine-year-old brother and my five-year-old sister to live with my father. This was a very tough time for us as children but it meant that I turned very quickly from a little girl into a mother figure to my siblings and to my father. By the age of eight I had learnt to cook, clean and do the washing, as I just wanted to make everything as normal as possible for my siblings. This difficult experience taught me that, no matter how many milestones we have to cross, the most important thing to remember is that anything is achievable if you approach it in the correct way – listening and trying and turning negatives into positives. My ambition as I grew up was to try to help other families wherever I could, and I feel honoured that I have achieved, and continue to achieve, this lifelong goal.

Over the last 15 years I have been privileged to work with people from all walks of life – from politicians, supermodels, actors and actresses, to stay-at-home parents and single mums and dads – and the one thing I have learnt is that we all encounter the same problems when we become parents. Sometimes we let our emotions take over when it comes to our little ones, but it is so important on this journey to remain mentally and morally strong, and never be afraid to seek or ask for help or advice.

Personally, I could not wait to become a parent and I became a mother for the first time at the young age of 21. I now have three children – George, Hollie and Olivia – and, like all parents out there, have experienced the different challenges that being a parent brings. As parents we always want to do the best for our children and sometimes we can be harsh on ourselves if we feel this cannot be achieved. After all, children do not come with instructions! We are always learning, no matter what age our children are.

Potty training is no exception and can be one of the most difficult milestones that both parents and toddlers will face. Sometimes the pressure we feel to get our children out of nappies leads us to all too easily feel that we have failed. Rather than choosing the time wisely and preparing for the task, we rush into potty training purely to satisfy other people's – or society's – expectations.

Under a huge amount of pressure from friends and family, receiving comments such as 'I cannot believe he is still in nappies!', I started potty training my son George before I felt he was really ready. Even though he was only two years old and wasn't showing any signs of readiness, and my daughter Hollie was just two weeks old at the time, I did not want people to think I was a bad parent, and so I naively potty trained George with great difficulty. This decision turned my household into a very stressful one – not only for me, but also for my son. The icing on the cake came when I was out and about with George. He, like most toddlers, would only use his own familiar potty and, of course, when he needed to go ... he *needed* to go! When George finally got to the stage where he would ask to use his own potty in the high street, I could not believe the disgust and rude comments we received from some onlookers when they saw him use it. This was a total shock to me but, worst of all, it upset George, making him feel that he had done something wrong. This made our potty training situation a whole lot worse. Not only did it have an effect on George but, as a parent, I felt I had let him down and I vowed never again to let total strangers influence where or when my child would use their potty. I learnt to listen to my children rather than other people and I adopted a very different approach with my two daughters, waiting for them to show clear signs of readiness. This made the whole experience of potty training a much less stressful time for me and, most importantly, for my two girls.

I could not believe that potty training was surrounded by so much controversy and how many different opinions were shared among competitive friends. And this continues to be an issue today. In fact, even more so, with the presence of social media and Internet forums.

**Q**: My little one is two-and-a-half years old and she was two months premature. She has started to speak simple words, but is showing no signs of being ready for potty training. However, I am getting constant remarks and pressure from family members, asking why she is still in nappies when her cousin the same age is potty trained! What shall I do?

**A**: You know your daughter better than anyone. It is very easy for people to judge from the outside, but every parent will know if their child is ready for potty training. You have to take into consideration that your daughter was born two months early – this can cause a delay in some of her developmental milestones. This does not mean there is anything wrong with her, just that she is not yet ready due to her being premature. As a parent you will always get others comparing their child to yours or offering you 'good advice', but remember that you will know when the time is right and your child starts showing signs of readiness (see page 29). Be assured that you, as her parent, will only do what is best for your daughter. And whether you feel the time is right or not this is your decision and nobody else's. Do not feel pressured and push potty training as this will only impact on your little one's eventual success.

My personal experiences really taught me how this difficult milestone can have a huge impact on the whole family. Determined to make life easier for everyone, I made it my mission to develop some amazing solutions to make potty training fun and magical for both parents and toddlers, and, importantly, to change the perception of doom and gloom we can all so easily adopt when faced with getting our children out of nappies.

After extensive research and working with many different families, I discovered that the biggest initial challenge was getting the toddler to engage with their potty. This gave me my first light bulb moment and I invented the My Carry Potty® – the world's only leakproof potty. By adding animal characters, my aim was to develop a potty that children could be captivated by and take ownership of – I wanted them to feel like it was their own special potty. The My Carry Potty® has a handle to encourage little ones to want to carry it everywhere with them, meaning they only use one potty in and out of the home. Not only does the potty become their own personal possession, they will never get caught short when out and about again. When developing the My Carry Potty®, the most important thing I learnt was that the child must feel comfortable or even excited about using the potty. Creating this bond between the child and *their* potty has made potty training so much more fun, but has also taken the stress out of it for parents worldwide!

Recognising that fun and consistency are the key elements of potty training, I set up The Potty Training Academy for nursery schools and parents. I developed a master training pack for nursery schools and key workers, as well as a mini pack for parents to use at home, to give toddlers a consistent programme to help with the whole potty training process. This has been a huge success with little ones around the globe, and it has helped countless key workers, giving them the confidence and consistency to potty train children in their care. I am very proud that my programme is not only encouraging little ones out of nappies and becoming confidently school-ready, but also reducing the huge amount of excess nappies being dumped in landfills across the globe.

Twenty years on, I am still working very closely with the education sector, including child psychologists and paediatricians, as well as visiting families in their homes using my fun and magical programme to successfully potty train a huge number of toddlers. I have worked with hundreds of different families in the UK and worldwide – in places as far-flung as the UAE, Australia, New Zealand, the USA and the Mediterranean – dealing with many different cultures and the ways they have been taught to potty train their little ones. For example, in some parts of China they use a nappy called the 'split crotch', which has a split in the middle to allow the toddler to wee or poo without having to pull their nappy/pants down. In Vietnam they choose a very different approach where the parents or grandparents – and sometimes even older siblings – hold the toddler over a potty and make a gentle whistling sound so the child then begins to associate this with the need to wee until they can do it on their own. In most Mediterranean countries – and I know this from experience as I am half-Maltese – children are generally potty trained by the time they are two-and-a-half. This is partly because children attend every event, day or night, and parents do not like the embarrassment of their child not being potty trained, and partly because grandparents and extended family have a massive influence on a toddler's upbringing so they all get involved and help out.

No matter where in the world I have been, teaching my potty training formula has proven to be 100 per cent successful. My expertise in this field has led me to become the UK's award-winning potty and toddler training expert, a regular expert on ITV's *This Morning* and many other parenting programmes, and a frequent contributor to the press and radio internationally. I am also well-known in the high-profile celebrity world, being called on by many to help with their toddler milestones, such as potty training, eating habits, preparing for school and behaviour.

When you start potty training you can be faced with many challenges, such as regression, refusal to potty train, difficulties potty training when out and about, bed-wetting, night-time training, diarrhoea, constipation, nappy rash and much more. Not to mention the emotional pressure this milestone can have on a family. My aim with this book is to give you helpful, practical advice on every eventuality you may encounter and help you to overcome any challenges you may be faced with along the way.

I believe the key to my successful potty training programme is seeing the experience through the toddler's eyes. Understanding the way your child thinks and feels will help you as parents make the process more engaging and fun rather than the stressful approach many of us expect.

I want this book to make you feel that I am holding your hand throughout the whole potty training journey, giving you 100 per cent confidence to start this next milestone and successfully potty train your little one. It is my hope that, by sharing my 20 years of knowledge with you, I can help you turn this into a fun and magical experience. I believe we can do it together. Let's ditch those nappies for good and make potty training MAGIC!

# 1 Welcome to *My* World of Potty Training

D id you know that in the 1950s children were potty trained as early as 18 months? This was due to the fact that disposable nappies were not yet around and parents had the tough job of washing terry towelling nappies, which consisted of a towelling nappy, a pin and plastic nappy pants over the top. Once soiled they had to be soaked in buckets until they were washed, which let off a very strong smell (I can still smell the stench from my childhood!). The nappies then had to be boiled before they could be reused. Toddlers had to be changed more often as they would feel uncomfortable and insist on a change, even soaking their parents' arms when being carried! All this hard work is the main reason that little ones were potty trained so early.

In 1946 a woman called Marion Donovan from Indiana was so fed up with the task of changing her daughter's cloth diapers because of all the mess it made on her clothing and bedding that she took out her sewing machine and a shower curtain and developed the first waterproof diaper cover, which not only kept clothing and bedding dry, but also significantly reduced nappy rash and did not pinch the child's skin. In 1949, after refusals from several different manufacturers, Saks 5th Avenue decided to trial the diaper cover and it soon became hugely successful. Donovan then took to creating a disposable nappy using a special paper lining that was strong and absorbent and kept water away from the baby's skin. She took her latest invention to every large manufacturer in America and, once again, was refused by all of them. It was not until 10 years later, in 1961, that a man called Victor Mills saw the benefit of Donovan's invention and created Pampers®.

In 1947 a British woman called Valerie Hunter-Gordon also created a disposable nappy as a result of the huge mess and washing she encountered after having her third child. Her nappy system, called Paddi, used nylon parachutes, tissues, wadding and cotton wool. Hunter-Gordon started off making these disposable nappies at home and supplying all her friends, while testing and modifying her design. She then applied for a patent and had the nappies mass produced in 1949. At first most parents were quite resistant to the nappies as the general public were not used to throwing things away in the post-war years. However, confidence soon grew and Hunter-Gordon was elated when Boots started selling her product and it became popular across the UK and the US.

Now, in the twenty-first century, we are throwing away a staggering number of disposable nappies every day. In the UK we are disposing of 8 million nappies per day equating to 3 billion per year! This is enough to fill 70,000 double-decker buses which, if they were parked one in front of the other, would be enough to stretch from London to Edinburgh! In the US a massive 49 million nappies are being thrown away per day, which is a huge 20 billion per year! And did you know that the average parent will use up to 5500 nappies until their child is three-and-a-half years old, costing parents in the UK £1400, which equates to £33 per month? Not to mention the shocking fact that it costs the government – and therefore the taxpayer – £40 million per year to dispose of them.

In addition to all this, there are the environmental issues that disposable nappies bring. They are all ending up in landfills and take hundreds of years to decompose. As they do so the faeces in them releases a greenhouse gas called methane, contributing to climate change. In fact, the number of disposable nappies used in just one child's life accounts for as much as 630kg of methane – which is as much as a car would generate over 1800 miles. And let's not forget the 200,000 trees per year it takes to produce disposable nappies in the US alone!

Because nappies are so much more absorbent now and advanced technology means that toddlers do not notice when they are wet, they do not feel the need to come out of them, which has led to an overall delay in potty training. Today, the average age of potty training is three to three-and-a-half years old, which has almost doubled since the 1950s, and unfortunately is still rising worldwide. I have seen that delayed potty training is on the increase leading to children starting their Reception year wearing disposable nappies/pull-ups underneath their school uniforms. This then leads to health issues such as constipation and urinary tract infections, which in turn lead to tummy pains, as children tend to hold in their wee or poo because they are not fully toilet trained, have no confidence or are afraid to ask to go to the toilet in front of all their friends. This is why it is so important that children are potty trained before they start school. Aside from the physical issues with delayed potty training, there are social and emotional impacts too, which can lead to children missing out on social activities, such as sports or sleepovers, as they lack the confidence to be away from home in case of an accident. This can also lead to bullying which can further hinder a child's self-esteem and education. I strongly feel this needs to change and we as parents can do something about it.

# Potty Training Myths

When it comes to potty training, everyone has an opinion and there is so much advice out there that parents are often left feeling daunted and confused. Many parents I have worked with have tried a variety of techniques to potty train their child, which has resulted in pitfalls and misunderstandings.

Before we begin, I think it's important to dispel some common potty training myths that may interfere with your chances of successfully potty training your child. I have listed below the most common misconceptions I have encountered over the years:

## You should only potty train in the spring or summer

There is a myth that it's best to potty train in the spring and summer so your toddler can run around with no clothes on, but this is simply not the case. When your toddler is showing all the signs they are ready (see page 29), come rain or snow you have to begin. It is not sensible or plausible to expect little ones to wait until the summer arrives before starting to potty train! This myth really drives me mad as all this is going to do is delay your toddler and make your life more difficult.

> **Q**: My son has started telling me when he is doing a wee and a poo and wants his nappy off immediately. He has also got into the habit of taking his nappy off himself and handing it to me. He is a very bright little boy and I think he is ready to start potty training, but as it is winter time I have been told to wait until the summer when it is warmer. What is your advice please?

> **A**: It is amazing to hear that your little boy is showing all the signs he is ready to start potty training. You must go with this and not wait many months for the summer to arrive – there is no season for potty training. This is a great opportunity that cannot be missed. If you delay training until the summer you may find that your son shows no interest whatsoever, which will make potty training a lot more difficult for you both.

## It is better to leave toddlers pants-free when potty training

This is a myth that many of the parents I work with have been told. Though going pants-free is great when toddlers are simply playing outside in the summer, in my experience it is so important that little ones get used to wearing pants from the outset of potty training so that they are able to recognise the difference between wearing a nappy/pull-up (and therefore the security of any wee or poo being 'caught') and big boy/girl pants. If you potty train your toddler wearing no pants, once you try to introduce big boy/girl pants further down the line they will associate this with the same sense of security they had when wearing a nappy/pull-up, which can lead to regular accidents, and you will often have to start the training again from scratch.

## Boys are harder to train than girls

I have trained equal amounts of boys and girls, hundreds in fact. I have never experienced any different results between boys and girls and have always found there is little or no difference at all. The only time I have found a difference is when a parent will insist on their little boy learning to potty train standing up. This can cause a delay simply because there is more for the boy to think about and, initially, children have very little warning that they need to wee which can lead to more accidents.

## Potty training should be done by the time your child is 24 months old

There is no set time or age to start potty training. If your little one is showing no signs they are ready, success will not be achievable. Some toddlers will show signs of readiness before others, but putting pressure on your toddler and yourself when they are not ready will only delay the process. So many parents feel that when their toddler reaches two years of age they have to get rid of nappies/pull-ups, but this is not the case. You as the parent know your toddler better than anyone else, so do not rush unnecessarily.

## If your toddler is dry in the day they will be dry at night

Potty training in the day is completely separate to night-time training. Just because your toddler is dry in the day doesn't mean they will automatically be dry at night. I always teach my parents to get their toddler completely dry for a few months in the day before even attempting night-time training. Night-time training can take weeks, sometimes months, but this is totally normal (see page 90 for more on this).

## Once you start potty training there is no going back

This is a myth that I hear so many times! If you have started potty training and given it a good couple of weeks and your toddler is showing no interest and having lots of accidents then they are simply not ready. Have a break for one or two months and revisit the training with a fresh start.

## Elimination communication

Elimination communication (EC) is where parents potty train their baby straight from birth without using nappies. Parents start by observing what their baby does when they need to go for a wee or poo. They look out for facial expressions, squirming or crying and, when they have discovered what to look out for, the parent begins to make sounds such as 'Psss psss' for weeing and 'Hmm hmm' for pooing. Eventually the child associates these sounds with weeing and pooing and the parent can then use them to let their little one know that they are somewhere where they can 'eliminate' (do a wee or poo).

Lots of parents who have chosen this method have been very pleased with the results, with babies being dry within a year. Many feel that it gives them an instant bond like no other. It also saves on nappies, which helps the environment and your purse, and is cleaner for the baby as they won't be sitting in a soiled nappy.

Other parents have said that they found EC too much hard work and messy and have given up early, reverting to the more traditional method of potty training. Also, if you have a new baby, and are breastfeeding or dealing with colic, it can make it more difficult to recognise what the signals are. EC requires a long and big commitment from both parents and therefore isn't suitable for those parents who return to work early and rely on nurseries for childcare.

Through my years of potty training I like to see little ones develop and, when they reach potty training age, to be able to understand and go to the toilet independently without being lifted. I have trained a handful of children that had EC training at an early age but went on to regress as toddlers as they were waiting to be lifted and did not fully grasp the concept of going alone. Understanding their bodily functions is such an important part of a toddler's development and independence, but as a baby this is something they do not recognise and have no control over.

I strongly feel that parents have a right to choose whatever potty training method they wish and nobody should judge. I really admire any parent that perseveres with EC as it takes a huge amount of commitment. I personally feel that in today's world most of us are working, leading very busy lives and sometimes have multiple children. To add EC to the mix is something that would impact a family considerably, so if EC is what you feel is correct for you as a family and you lead busy lives, consider it carefully as it takes complete dedication.

# My Philosophy

As a mother of three, my approach to potty training is designed specifically for parents who feel their children are ready to be potty trained but do not want their child to be distressed or harmed by the process. I believe that potty training doesn't have to be traumatic for either the parent or the child, and the child has to feel secure, safe and happy in order to train successfully.

Potty training is something every parent has to embark on, and each and every child develops at a different rate so please concentrate on your own child and take no notice of the super parent who supposedly had their child toilet trained at birth. As a parent you will know when your child is ready. Try not to feel under pressure from other people and what society is preaching. It's important that you watch and listen to your little one and go with their pace, which will make potty training much more enjoyable for you both.

After several attempts with many different methods, I have discovered that toddlers always gravitate towards an organised, exciting and consistent approach. My philosophy is based on fun and seeing it through your toddler's eyes. It is so important to approach potty training in a way that you feel your toddler will positively respond to and that will keep them interested, making sure it's an enjoyable time for them. My programme makes potty training a fun and exciting experience rather than a military operation. It enables you to get down to your toddler's level and make the whole process a magical journey. This in turn will give you the results you want.

## Rewarding and praise

I am a great believer that a reward system should be put in place at the beginning of potty training. Rewarding and lots of praise is something we all love in life. I feel strongly that, from the outset of potty training, it is so important to really encourage our little ones to achieve success as much as possible and, unfortunately, as they get older just clapping hands and saying well done doesn't excite them enough.

The most commonly used reward system for toddlers is a weekly chart with stickers for every day of the week. This is a simple reward system that all children understand and is easy to follow. The chart can be made at home together (which means parents you need to get your creative hat on!) or purchased in store or online. (See page 40 for more on my approach.)

I have also created a fantastic unique reward system which parents and children love using – the magic reward box. This system uses named reward stars, a magic reward box and three magical prizes which can be earned as your child achieves their stars. (See page 40 for more on this.) The magic reward box works so effectively because it teaches toddlers to work towards something – to fill the box with stars to achieve their magical prize – and it also helps with other areas of their development, such as learning to count, patience, realising that their efforts bring rewards, and also having the determination to succeed, which will result in successful potty training. Every day is different with little ones, but letting them put their own stars in the magic reward box and wishing to get more is a unique technique that keeps toddlers constantly engaged – and it really works! The magic reward box can be used on its own or alongside the standard sticker chart. Many parents I have worked with have offered their little one a sticker for asking for the potty/toilet and a star in the box for doing a wee or poo as it provides a bit of variation.

It is important that you explain your chosen reward system to your child and make it very clear as and when they will get their stickers/stars. I always like to reward my little trainers for their efforts – asking for the potty/toilet – as well as for their achievements – actually going for a wee or poo. Avoid making the reward system too complicated as your little one will have enough to learn with the training itself, so make it fun and easy for them to understand.

## Language and emotion

It is very important that you use words of encouragement when you are potty training even if your little one has an accident or doesn't quite do what you have asked them to do. Try to always sound positive no matter what is thrown at you and always look your toddler in the eye when you praise them. And remember, a smile is worth a thousand words. (See page 70 for examples of language to use when rewarding and praising your little trainer.)

### A little note for the grown-ups

I have learnt over the years that potty training is a learning process for parents so it is as important that you understand all elements of this milestone as well as your toddler. Please try to follow every section of this book from start to finish (and repeat if necessary) to achieve the successful result you are looking for.

Every element of this book will help you to introduce a consistent, enjoyable experience for your toddler, and also for yourself. Let's get going!

# 2 Before We Start

Before you start on my programme, I want to share with you some experiences you may come across on your potty training journey, as well as offering some helpful tips and advice to make things easier along the way.

## Let's Talk Wee and Poo

Children's bladders develop at different rates, but most children will go through the following developmental stages:

- Under 1 year of age: no control over bowel or bladder movements.
- 1–1½ years: still little control.

- 2–3 years: most little ones should have more bladder control.
- 3–4 years: toddlers should have gained complete control.

If your little one doesn't follow this pattern, please don't worry. This is just a guide and toddlers all develop at different rates. However, if you are really worried that your little one is not developing as you feel they should or you feel that something is not quite right, then please seek further advice from your doctor or health visitor.

## Wee

On average toddlers should wee four to eight times a day, though this obviously depends on how much they have had to drink and how active they have been. It is really important for a healthy bladder and bowel to make sure that your little one drinks plenty of fluid throughout the day. Try to avoid caffeine-based drinks, such as tea, coffee or hot chocolate, and fizzy, sugary drinks, such as cola and lemonade, as these can make the bladder overactive, leading to accidents. The best drink to offer your toddler is water. Water will properly hydrate your toddler and quench their thirst without all the added sugars. Milk is also an important drink for little ones, providing essential calcium, protein and vitamin D, which are all important for growing bodies.

When you are potty training your child, don't limit their drinks during the day – the bladder needs to be exercised by being full and then emptied to encourage a healthy bladder. You can tell if your little one is drinking enough fluid by the colour of their wee:

- Pale yellow is a good colour and indicates that they are hydrated.
- Dark yellow is a sign that they are not drinking enough fluid and need to drink more.

It is also important to encourage your little one to take their time when having a wee to ensure that they fully empty their bladder as leftover wee may cause an infection (see page 133).

## Poo

From the age of two, children tend to stop pooing in their nappy/pull-up at night and will do this during the day. Often it is a lot harder getting toddlers to do a poo in the potty/toilet than it is getting them to do a wee. It is so important, therefore, to encourage a healthy bowel and avoid constipation as this can cause your toddler discomfort and delay potty training. It can even make your toddler frightened to let go. Fluid also plays a huge part in a healthy bowel as does keeping your little one active as physical activity really helps to get things moving down there.

Your toddler's diet is very important to keep their bowel healthy. Try to introduce vegetables, wholegrain foods – such as brown bread, brown rice, rice cakes and cereals such as Weetabix or porridge – and fruit into their daily menu. Make sure you don't just give your little one a diet high in wholegrain though as it can fill them up too easily, meaning they won't eat other important foods that contain protein and nutrients, so keep their diet balanced. (See Chapter 8 for more on this.)

## Tips for keeping wee and poo behaving

- Plenty of fluid. Keep your toddler hydrated to keep their bladder and bowel working and healthy.
- Cotton pants. These are the best to use on toddlers while they are potty training as nylon pants can promote the growth of bacteria and lead to infections. Make sure they are changed regularly.
- Cleanliness. Keep all your toddler's down-below areas clean with daily washing, using non-perfumed soap or bubbles.
- Regularly change nappies/pull-ups. If you are using nappies/pull-ups don't let your child sit in a wet or soiled one for long periods as this can cause infections and nappy rash.
- Balanced diet. Give your child a healthy, balanced diet with lots of fibre and plenty of vegetables and fruit to avoid constipation.

# Hygiene

I cannot stress enough how important it is to teach your child hygiene from a young age as this will have an impact throughout their early years. Hygiene is a key part of your child's development, and teaching them the importance of hand-washing when they are old enough and mobile enough to understand, will help to avoid common illnesses such as diarrhoea, colds, flu and stomach bugs.

I always explain to toddlers the importance of hand-washing, why it is necessary and what can happen if they do not do it. Each time your little trainer sits on the potty/toilet you must take them to wash their hands, even if they don't actually do a wee or poo as this instils good habits.

For the first few days of potty training you should teach your toddler how to wash their hands properly so that, as the days go on, they can do so independently. Make sure they use hand soap, lather between their fingers, rinse with warm water and dry their hands. Proper hand-washing is so important as we carry so many germs on our hands and, because little ones tend to hold on to the potty or toilet seat for support when they start potty training, germs can easily spread and make them poorly.

Common illnesses can be avoided by teaching toddlers this basic skill from the start, so let's get them washing their hands and wash those dirty germs away!

Remember not to leave little ones unattended with water as toddlers love playing with it and can get carried away – a flooded bathroom is not what you need at this time! You should also supervise your little one's hand-washing to avoid them turning on the hot tap and scalding themselves. It's a good idea to check the temperature setting on your boiler to make sure the water is not so hot that it is going to scald little hands.

## The wipe!

Once your little trainer has done their business on the potty/toilet, especially poos (and this relates to both sexes), it is important to teach them to wipe from front to back from day one. For girls, in particular, there is a chance of infection as their bottom is so close to their urethra and germs can travel up into the bladder, so wiping from front to back can help to avoid this happening. You may wish to use disposable wet wipes, but please be aware of the environmental impact and always look for the biodegradable sign on the packet. Wiping will take some time for your toddler to learn and you may have to assist for a while, even once they are potty trained!

It is also important to show girls how to wipe after they have been for a wee – again, from front to back. They all love doing this so it should not be a struggle! You can assist at the beginning, but gradually let her do this independently, but try to avoid her overwiping as this may cause her to be sore down below. Be warned, little girls tend to love using a lot of toilet roll for this! For boys you can use a tissue to dab the end of their penis or teach them to shake when they start standing to do a wee.

### A little note for the grown-ups

Getting your little one into a regular routine of washing their hands before eating and after going to the toilet is very important and is something that will stay with them throughout their life. And, don't forget, it is important for mummies and daddies to wash their hands too!

# Signs of Readiness

I t is vital to start potty training when your toddler is showing the correct signs they are ready to begin. Every child is unique and will display these signs at different rates. You know your toddler better than anyone else, so try not to compare them with others as this may only delay the process or add stress to you both. If your toddler is not showing any of the signs below and you choose to start potty training because they have had the odd fluke of using the potty/toilet but it is not consistent, they will end up regressing. There is no set age when to start potty training, but your toddler's ability to recognise the difference between wet and dry is a key initial sign.

Other signs that your toddler is ready to start potty training include:

- **Longer periods with dry nappies/pull-ups** indicate your toddler's bladder has developed stronger muscles which will lead to fewer accidents. If you notice your little one is staying dryer throughout the day, you are using fewer nappies/pull-ups and they are waking up dry after their daytime nap, this is a good sign they are ready to start. If your toddler no longer naps during the day, then keep an eye out for dryer nappies when they wake up in the morning.
- **Stopping in their tracks when they have done a wee or poo.** This is a key sign that your toddler knows what they are doing and recognises their bodily functions.
- **Insisting on a nappy change once they have soiled their nappy/pull-up** shows your toddler recognises the wetness or the poo and feels uncomfortable. This shows they are developing their understanding of the difference between what being dirty and clean feels like.

- **Starting to show independence in dressing and undressing** indicates your toddler is moving on to the next stage in their development from baby to toddler. They can pull their clothes up and down and show an interest in dressing and undressing. By this stage they may even want to choose their favourite clothes.

- **Understanding simple instructions and commands**, for example 'Go and get your shoes', or being able to go and get an object and bring it back to you is also key. If your toddler is unable to understand simple instructions it will be very difficult to successfully potty train them.

- **Being able to communicate** is also very important so that your toddler can tell you when they need a wee or poo. It is so important to use the words 'wee' and 'poo' with your child so that they associate these with what they are doing. As a parent, when you can see they are doing something in their nappy/pull-up, it's important you say to them 'Are you doing a wee or a poo?' even a few weeks prior to starting potty training.

**Q:** I started potty training my son after Christmas when he was just over two-and-a-half. I successfully potty trained my other son (now aged six) in a matter of days, so I assumed it would be the same for my youngest. No such luck! He is not afraid to use the potty or toilet and goes happily, but only if directed by me. He never tells me when he needs to go, and if I turn my back he is quite happy playing with poo in his pants or sitting in wet trousers, not even telling me after the event. He just doesn't seem to know about his bodily functions!

**A**: Every child is different, though I understand it can be quite easy to compare siblings. On this occasion your son does not appear to be showing full signs of readiness. These need to be apparent before any toddler will be willing to start potty training or can even understand what is happening. I would give potty training a break for now and revisit it in a month or so, but in the meantime I would advise you to start educating your son on potty training by reading books, using apps and showing him potty training flashcards (see page 40 and 45).

If your little one is showing all or most of the key signs that they're ready, let's begin trying to get those nappies/pull-ups off!

# 3 Getting Ready

I always say that preparation is key, and this is particularly true when you start potty training. Being organised by choosing the correct equipment and timing to suit your little one will make all the difference in making your potty training journey fun and successful.

## Essential Items

So, you are all ready to get started and your toddler is showing the signs of readiness outlined on page 29. Now all you need is to get organised! Pick a day when you are free to go out and get all of the essentials and let your little one know that you are going on a big adventure together to get some big girl/boy pants and a potty and/or trainer seat. It is so important that you make a big deal about this so that your toddler feels involved and excited from the start. On the way to your chosen store, tell them again where you are going and encourage them to repeat it back to you – this is all part of the exciting build-up. Make this a special magical day with a lunch treat afterwards so it is an occasion that your little one will remember.

Once you reach the store, it is imperative that you let your toddler choose which potty/trainer seat they would like and also which big girl/boy pants they want. After all, it is them being trained. Obviously bear in mind that some potties/trainer seats can be quite pricey so make sure you do a little research before you arrive and only show your toddler the options available within your budget! If you do not have a store close by, shopping online can also be fun. But remember, letting your little one have a say or choosing their own potty/trainer seat is key.

## Potty

Let your little one choose their own potty, within reason. Make sure the options you offer your child are within your budget, but it is important to let them have one that they are excited about – perhaps one with their favourite animal or Disney character on or just one in their favourite colour. There are so many to choose from but it is essential to get your toddler involved. There are many slightly less costly potties which you can let your little one customise themselves with their favourite stickers.

It is important not to choose a huge potty as I always advise you to take your potty out with you wherever you go so your toddler is not caught short. Little ones like to stick with the one potty they are familiar with, so there is no need to spend a fortune on lots of different potties, though you may wish to buy two of the same potty – one for upstairs and one for downstairs – but this is not essential.

Once you've bought the potty, you need to decide where your little trainer would like to position it. Some parents I have worked with have insisted on the potty being placed in the bathroom so that any accidents or mess can be easily cleaned up, but I always follow the toddler's lead on this as it needs to be somewhere that is visual to remind them it is there and easily accessible for quick use. Your child has been in nappies/pull-ups from birth and is used to weeing and pooing in their nappy/pull-up with no effort, so it is unrealistic to, all of a sudden, expect them to stop what they are doing and go and find their potty when they might be at the other end of the house. This may lead to accidents.

If the potty is in a bedroom or another room that has carpet, you may want to place it on a towel to help protect the carpet from any possible accidents or spills. It's important that, to begin with at least, the potty is placed in a room where your little one spends most of their time. It can be moved into the bathroom area after a week or two when you feel your little one has gained potty training confidence and the ability to hold on for long enough to get there.

You may choose not to purchase a potty if you want to train your little one straight on the toilet (see below).

## Trainer seat

A trainer seat reduces the size of the toilet by making it less daunting for your toddler to sit on. Make sure you choose one that fits your toilet correctly and read the reviews beforehand. If it does not fit the toilet properly, children can pinch their fingers when the seat moves, which can make some toddlers feel uneasy about using it.

You may decide to train your little one straight on the toilet, or the trainer seat can also be used for the transition from potty to toilet, so it's always great to have one from the start for when your little one is completely confident. Trainer seats can also be taken with you when you are out and about.

Try to get a matching trainer seat that is the same colour or design as your potty for consistency. You can also use your toddler's favourite character stickers to decorate the plainer, less expensive seats.

## Potty versus trainer seat

Parents often ask me whether they should use a potty or a trainer seat when potty training their little one. I have found that most of my little trainers gravitate towards a potty to begin with as it is smaller and closer to the ground, which makes it easier for them to use and is less intimidating than climbing up on to a big toilet. A potty is also quicker for your little one to access if they are in a hurry to go, plus it is easier to take a potty with you when you are out and about.

Trainer seats are generally used when your little one is ready to progress from the potty to the toilet. They are very useful in helping to alleviate the fear your little one may have of falling into the big toilet by creating a smaller open area and making them feel secure. Trainer seats can be used for as long as it takes for your little one to be ready to transition to the big toilet and toddlers generally use them without any fuss.

If budget allows, it's always helpful to have both a potty and a trainer seat to hand. Try choosing a seat that matches your child's potty in colour or design as this keeps training consistent and will help make the transition to the toilet smoother.

## Big girl/boy pants

Buying big girl/boy pants in advance of starting potty training is essential as you'll need to start putting these on your toddler from day one. Again, it is really important to let your toddler choose their favourite colours or characters, obviously within reason. Make sure you purchase at least 20 pairs of pants as accidents will happen – look around for the best price so that you have plenty of spares to hand as they will be needed! Try to stick to good-quality soft cotton pants and avoid cheap nylon ones as you don't want your little one to be uncomfortable and give them an excuse not to wear them.

Once you've purchased the big girl/boy pants, it's important to sit down and explain to your toddler what the difference is between the nappy/pull-up they are wearing and these special pants. Use simple language and an explanation such as, 'These pants are for big girls/boys just like you and nappies/pull-ups are now for little babies. Mummy/Daddy cannot wait to see you wear these big girl/boy pants. It will make me very happy.'

## Step stool

A step stool is invaluable for little ones. Stools have so many uses – from helping little ones reach the toilet, to helping them to reach the sink to wash their hands or clean their teeth. But the main benefit they have for toilet training is that they create the correct squat position. This is where the child's legs are kept slightly raised because their feet are placed on the stool, it is the most natural position to be in when doing a poo as it helps to release it. This is particularly helpful if toddlers are suffering with constipation (see page 140).

Make sure the stool has a non-slip bottom and do not leave your little ones unattended on the stool, particularly the younger ones.

**Correct squat position**

## Potty training storybook/app

Reading potty training stories to your little trainer will really help them to understand what potty training is all about. Just because your toddler is showing signs they are ready, does not mean that they understand what potty training actually is.

Start introducing the book daily for about a week prior to you starting. A good time to read these stories is at bedtime so that you have your child in a calm place with their undivided attention. Read the book every night and get your toddler involved by asking them questions about the story. In my experience, this is a great way to teach children the basics before they begin as it reinforces the steps and helps your toddler understand what is going to happen.

There are also many apps/animations available now which have a potty training story and children love these. They help to communicate the message you need to get across and encourage your toddler when the training begins. These can be purchased from iTunes or through an app store.

## Reward chart and stickers

Rewards are essential for extra encouragement when your child is potty training. Choose a nice big chart with the days of the week on it with squares big enough to accommodate some magical stickers. Reward charts are readily available to purchase online or in store – there are plenty of free charts that can be downloaded too – and can also be made at home. If you choose to make the chart yourself, buy an A3 piece of card, draw a grid with the days of the week on it and help your child to personalise the chart using stars or their favourite character stickers. Don't forget to put your toddler's name at the top so they know that the chart belongs to them. This is a fun exercise to do with your little trainer prior to starting potty training and will really help them to grasp a good understanding of how to use it. See page 191 for an example reward chart.

Position the reward chart in the room in which your toddler spends most of their day – usually the kitchen or living room – and make sure they can reach it. The chart has to be visible as a constant reminder. I believe it is important to reward toddlers with a sticker just for trying as this is a great step forward, so reward your little one with a sticker when they ask to go on the potty/toilet. Always use powerful words such as, 'Well done for asking – you are such a big girl/boy' as this makes toddlers feel very special. When your toddler actually does a wee or poo, reward them with two stickers for a wee and three stickers for a poo, as this makes it extra special. Use lots of exciting praise like, 'Wow, you have done a wee/poo and you have made Mummy/Daddy very happy!' along with a clap. Keep praising your little one throughout the day and remind them that the chart and special stickers are waiting for them. At the end of each day do a 'Big Count' together – count the stickers on the chart with your little trainer and show them what they have achieved. Sharing the chart with the rest of the family is also extra special too.

## Magic reward box and jar of stars

In all my years of potty training toddlers, I have used a magic reward box to add an extra element of surprise to further encourage the child. This system uses named reward stars in a choice of your child's favourite colour and a magic reward box with a hole in the top big enough for little hands to drop their reward stars in. The stars can be made on a computer with your child's name on, and you could let them decorate them to add an extra element of fun. You can either buy a magic reward box or make one at home (see page 192 for an example magic reward box). You'll also need a clear small jar for the stars to go in. The idea is that when your toddler has used the potty/toilet they can take a star out of the jar and place it in their magic reward box.

Keep the magic reward box and jar of stars up high so your toddler cannot reach them, but low enough that they can still see them. Wrap up three presents in the same colour paper as the stars. Place a large star with the numbers 5, 10 and 15 on the front of each gift and place them on the shelf next to the magic reward box so they are clearly visible. When your toddler has achieved the amount of stars on the front of the presents, they will receive their magical prize. This could be taking them to their favourite place, an activity or simply a small toy. This creates an extra element of surprise and is a great system for further encouragement.

When your little trainer asks to go on the potty/toilet they will receive a star – this is key to getting your toddler to ask and is a really important step in my programme. Your toddler will gain two stars if they do a wee on the potty/toilet and three stars if they do a poo. For extra encouragement, halfway through the day count how many stars your toddler has achieved and let them know how many more they need to get in order to receive their magical prize. At the end of each day, as part of your daily routine, do a 'Big Count' together. Toddlers really enjoy sitting with Mummy/Daddy and counting how many stars they have achieved in the day. This makes them feel super special and is key to keeping the encouragement going. Every toddler I have ever worked with has become beyond excited by this!

I always advise never to get angry or cross when potty training but I have used the removal of a star or sticker for deliberate accidents and it has worked. I have only implemented this if I thought it was necessary and definitely not in the first week of training.

You may wish to use just one reward system, but you can use both a reward chart and stickers alongside a magic reward box. For example, you could use a sticker when your child asks for the potty/toilet and a star when your child actually goes, to make it more magical.

If your little trainer is going to their grandparents' house, nursery or out and about, you need to keep the rewards consistent. Take two clear sandwich bags with you – one for transporting the magic stars/stickers and one for the magic stars/stickers to be put into once your little one has earned them. When you return home the stickers can be put on the chart or the stars can be popped into the magic reward box. It is so important to maintain consistency in and out of the home wherever your toddler goes – this is a key element of my approach.

**Q**: My daughter has been doing great with potty training at nursery and never comes home with wet pants. However, once she's at home it's another story altogether. Most days, I pick her up from nursery and, before she goes to bed, I've changed her out of wet pants two or three times. I don't know how to encourage her to use the potty at home.

**A**: It's very common for little ones to do well in one environment but not so well in another. The possible reason your daughter is doing well at nursery is likely the result of a strict routine, with regular potty visits at specific times each day.

She may be more willing to go on the potty and has few or no accidents at nursery because she is doing so alongside her group of friends. Try introducing a reward system for when she is at home for further encouragement and to try to break this habit. This will give her a purpose. It would be great if you could have a set routine for when she gets back from nursery until this is sorted and don't forget to keep prompting her.

## Child-friendly hand soap

Get a nice squidgy hand soap to be used every time your toddler uses the potty/toilet. This really encourages and instils good hygiene habits at an early age and all children love water! There are so many products on the market but make sure the soap is child-friendly and not heavily scented.

## Flashcards

Potty training flashcards are a very effective way of enabling toddlers to understand and grasp what you are asking them to do and are a key part of my programme. If you show your child a picture of a girl/boy sitting on the potty/toilet, they will associate what you are teaching them with the visuals on the picture. I have always made flashcards part of my training routine as it adds some fun – your toddler will think it's a game, but it is also teaching them what a potty/toilet is actually used for. I find that showing toddlers visually where wee and poo belong gives them a much clearer understanding of what to do when I ask them to go on the potty/toilet.

Flashcards can be purchased very easily in store or online, or you can make them at home by downloading pictures, sticking them on to card and writing a simple description of what is happening in the picture on the reverse side. There are some ideas below on which images work well and see page 193 for some example flashcards.

- A girl/boy sitting on the potty/toilet.
- A girl/boy flushing the toilet.
- A girl/boy washing their hands.
- A special reward chart (this can be an image on a flashcard in addition to the actual reward chart).
- A special 'Well done!' (this can be a mummy/daddy giving a big star).
- A potty.
- A toilet.
- A nappy/pull-up.
- Big girl/boy pants.
- A wee in the potty.
- A poo in the potty.
- A wee in the toilet.
- A poo in the toilet.

# Little plastic bin for nappies/pull-ups

I make a point of putting a little plastic bin in the little one's bedroom so that every morning and after every nap they can put their nappy/pull-up in the bin themselves. This gives them the responsibility of making sure that they throw their nappy/pull-up in the bin before they put on their big girl/ boy pants. (Make sure you give your toddler's bottom a good wipe and ensure that they are clean and dry before they put on their big girl/boy pants and leave their bedroom.)

From now on, we want your little trainer to associate wearing a nappy/pull-up with sleep times only, and throwing their own nappy/pull-up in the bin will make them feel involved in the potty training process and teach them that it is 'goodbye to nappies/pull-ups for good'!

The bin can be a cheap one from a discount shop and you could even label it with your toddler's name: 'George's night-time nappy bin', for example.

## Potty training shopping list

- Potty.
- Trainer seat.
- Big girl/boy pants.
- Step stool.
- Potty training storybook/app.
- Reward chart (or materials to make one) and stickers.

- Magic reward box (or materials to make one), stars and clear jar.
- Child-friendly hand soap.
- Flashcards (or materials to make them).
- Little plastic bin.

Over the years I have used all of the above tools and they are hugely effective. Potty training doesn't have to be a costly process – shop around for the best deals; there are many stores and supermarkets that sell most of the above at very affordable prices. I believe that using all or some of these tools introduces fun and consistency and makes potty training a magical experience for your toddler. In my experience, turning potty training into an enjoyable experience in turn leads to successful toilet training.

# Dos and Don'ts of Potty Training

There are so many elements that can affect potty training, and when to start potty training is always the big question I get asked by parents. It's so important to ensure you choose the correct time and technique when potty training your little one in order to achieve successful results.

## Don't begin if there is a change in circumstances

It is not a good idea to start potty training if:

- Your toddler has been unwell.
- There is a new baby in the family.
- You have just moved into a new home.
- Your child has just started or changed nursery.
- There are any family problems within the household, such as a separation or death in the family.

Anything that changes a toddler's world – from the super exciting to more stressful situations – will affect them more than it will affect you. Toddlers love to feel secure in their surroundings so, if there has been a change in circumstances at home, it would be better to wait a month or two and let things settle down before you embark on potty training. However, you can still prepare your toddler by using the words 'wee' and 'poo', drawing their attention to it when they are clearly doing a wee or poo in their nappy/pull-up, and letting them see what is in their nappy/pull-up once they have done their business.

## Don't start too early

It is so easy to listen to other people's opinions and recommendations and feel under pressure to start potty training.

Starting too early when your toddler is not able to communicate, express their feelings or recognise their bodily functions can lead to failure. So make sure your little one is showing all the signs they are ready before you start (see page 29) and don't be influenced by what others preach.

## Don't put a time limit on it

It is important not to set your expectations too high and set a time limit on potty training. Some little ones can get the hang of it in days, while for others it may take weeks, or even months, to become dry. Rushing the process will only lead to regression, so take your time and success will follow.

## Don't become cross

Potty training can be very frustrating for both you and your toddler, but it's important to remember that it is a huge step for your toddler to suddenly remember unprompted to ask to use the potty/toilet. Little ones do not like to disappoint their parents, so try not to become cross with your child for accidents or not wanting to sit on the potty/toilet. Instead, turn your frustration into lots of encouragement using upbeat and happy language such as, 'Mummy/Daddy is so proud of you for trying' or 'What a big girl/boy you are, using the potty/toilet and wearing big girl/boy pants.' Don't forget: practise makes perfect.

## Do speak to your child about potty training before you start

It is always good to have a potty training storybook to read to your little trainer at least a week before you start. This will take them from the unknown and create an exciting build-up to the big day, giving them a desire to potty train and become a big girl/boy. When you can see that your toddler is doing a wee or poo in their nappy/pull-up, it's also important to say to them 'Are you doing a wee or a poo?'. This is really key as it helps little ones to understand and start to recognise their own bodily functions.

## Do start when your toddler is showing signs they are ready

Unless your circumstances are about to change, which may affect the consistent training, if your toddler is showing all or most of the key signs they are ready, outlined on page 29, do get started. There is no need to delay until spring or summer.

## Do transition from nappies/pull-ups to pants

Make sure you use big girl/boy pants and get those nappies/pull-ups off during the day. It is so important for your toddler to make that transition and to understand that they are now a big girl/boy and do not need nappies/pull-ups in the day anymore. Many parents tend to use nappies/pull-ups as well as pants to avoid accidents and for going out of the home, but I always train children with just pants – if a nappy/pull-up is used during training then it can make toddlers lazy and lead to accidents and regression as they know the nappy/pull-up is there for protection. Using both nappies/pull-ups and pants will only confuse your toddler and send very mixed messages.

## Do take your potty/trainer seat out and about with you

Trying to find a toilet quickly when you're out and about is sometimes tricky and, if your toddler has an accident outside the home, this can really knock their confidence. For the first few weeks of potty training it's a good idea to take your potty with you wherever you go as your toddler will normally give you very little notice that they need to go.

## Do talk to your childcare provider

Different childcare settings require different things in relation to potty training. Some will expect your child to be fully potty trained before they attend, while others are more relaxed about it and are happy to support your efforts at home. Speak to your childcare provider and discuss with them that you are about to start potty training. Inform them of the way you will be doing this and what programme you will be following, as well as how to reward or praise your little one. This must be kept consistent at all times.

## Do get the family involved

Speak to grandparents, aunties, uncles, etc. and make them aware that your little one is starting their potty training journey. This will create extra encouragement which is very special for your little trainer.

# The Day Before the Big Day

It's now time to get out your chosen reward system. If it is the magic reward box, find a shelf that it can be placed on and make sure you say to your toddler 'Wow, Mummy/ Daddy is putting your magic reward box on the shelf with your magic stars and this is just for you because you are going to be a big girl/boy.' Explain to your child how they can win a magic star and how many they will get for wees and poos. Make sure the magic reward box and clear jar of magic stars are on a shelf out of reach, but somewhere where they are clearly visible to your little one.

If you choose a reward chart introduce this to your little one today and explain to them how they will win a sticker. The chart must be placed somewhere where your child can reach it so they can put their stickers on the chart immediately after they have asked for the potty/ toilet or done a wee or poo.

Today is the time to run through with your toddler all that you have shown them over the last few days and ask them questions about all the different elements. This is a great exercise and a fun game for your little one that will help to give them a better understanding of what is expected of them. Let them know how excited you all are that they are starting potty training and what a 'special big girl/boy' they are going to be.

## A little word for the grown-ups

If you are a working parent, do not worry as all this preparation can be done in the evenings to suit you. It is just important that you teach and explain everything to your child before getting started.

Preparation before the big day is as important as the training itself, and being organised will make potty training a whole lot easier for you as a parent.

Try to avoid visitors tomorrow just so you and your little one can both find your feet and give this training a good kick-start together. Distractions on Day One can hinder your child's introduction to potty training and the first few days are important for you both to get used to a new routine.

Prepare for the week ahead by choosing loose, easily accessible clothing for your toddler, such as soft joggers or dresses that can be pulled up or down quickly. Avoid jeans and clothes with lots of buttons or drawstrings as this will only lead to accidents and make your little one very frustrated if they cannot undo their clothing quickly, they usually have very little or no warning that they need to go.

Lay out the big girl/boy pants in your toddler's room ready for the morning and let them choose which ones they want to wear when they wake up. Have plenty of pants ready as they may need lots tomorrow. You will normally get through quite a few on the first day.

Once you are all set up, walk around the house with your little trainer and get them to help you find their potty/trainer seat and reward chart/magic reward box; this makes it exciting and like a game. Ask them 'Where is your potty/trainer seat? Mummy/Daddy has forgotten!'

This is fun for them but also reminds them where everything is and will really help with the start tomorrow.

Run through the rewards one more time. Ask them:

- 'How many stars/stickers do you get for asking for the potty/ toilet?'
- 'How many stars/stickers do you get for a wee?'
- 'How many stars/stickers do you get for a poo?'
- 'How many stars/stickers do you think you will get tomorrow?'

It is always special to get your little trainer to FaceTime or call grandparents or other family members so they can join in the encouragement for the big day. Remember to pre-warn grandparents or other family members that the call from the little one is coming so they are ready and waiting.

This is a big day for you as parents too and can be quite overwhelming and very daunting. Accidents will happen and sometimes you will lose the will to live and wonder 'What am I doing? How are they ever going to get the hang of this?' I know it's hard sometimes, but try to stay calm and patient as your little one will get there in the end. Your little trainer is about to move on to the next stage of their development which is very exciting, and just think about all the money you are going to save on nappies/pull-ups! So a big 'Good luck' to you too.

# 4 Let's Begin

When I started my parenting journey I never imagined the rollercoaster of emotions I would feel during the different stages of my children's lives. From weaning to potty training, we all look out for the signs our little ones are ready and are told to 'go for it', but I'm not sure that we as parents ever consider whether *we* are emotionally ready and confident enough for the difficult tasks that lie ahead.

Potty training can certainly be challenging and is a task that takes a lot of consideration and preparation before the hard work even begins. As parents, we have to reassure ourselves that we do actually possess the energy to undertake potty training. Most of you may not have potty trained before, so you have to be realistic about what you can achieve, and don't expect too much of yourself. This way you will find it easier to enjoy this exciting stage rather than setting your expectations too high.

I always saw potty training my little ones as a great bonding opportunity as it's another time to notice what is unique and special about them. Potty training is a natural thing we all have to learn, and it is an incredibly important stage in your little one's life.

Take your time and work through the advice in Chapter 3 to prepare yourself before the big day. Being organised can really help take the pressure off. The most important thing you can do as a parent is to believe in yourself, so make sure you are in a good place and don't have any other major commitments; remember you are on this very special journey together. Be kind to yourself and take your time. This will make you strong and help build a beautiful relationship with your little one. Everything should then fall into place.

When you have decided to begin potty training I would recommend that you start at the weekend if you work during the week or if your child attends a childcare setting. This will give you two uninterrupted days to get started. A long weekend is even better. Potty training is a huge milestone and also a great bonding time, so I would encourage you to do this together as a family, if possible.

If your child is looked after by grandparents or attends a childcare setting, once you have kick-started potty training it is important to explain your programme to them so that they can keep the continuity going while your child is out of the house – consistency is a key part of my programme.

**Q**: My parents look after my son for two days a week. He is nearly three years old and is showing signs that he is ready to start potty training. How will being in two different houses affect his potty training?

**A**: When you are about to start potty training, try to have the first few days at home so you and your child can establish a routine together. This means that, after a few days, your son should begin to recognise the new routine and, most importantly, understand the rewards and what he is getting them for. It's so important to keep the continuity going once you begin potty training, so whatever routine and rewards you have established at home need to be continued when your son is with your parents. I would advise that you ask your parents to come over for a couple of hours to watch what you are doing so they can see what it is they have to do on the two days when they look after your son. This will ensure the routine is established and will keep it all consistent. Don't forget to take your son's potty/trainer seat to your parents' house on the two days they have him.

# Day One

The big day has arrived and you have everything prepared and in place, so let's do this!

Once your little trainer wakes up, take their nappy/pull-up off and get them to put it in the bin. When they have thrown the nappy/pull-up in the bin, say to them, 'Well done! You are such a big boy/girl for putting that sleep nappy/pull-up in the bin. Thank you.' Clean and dry their bottom, and then let them choose the big boy/girl pants they want to wear, reminding them that today they are 'a big boy/girl and are wearing big pants which is so exciting!'. Try to get your little trainer to put on their own pants (maybe with a little help from you) as it is important to encourage independence over the next few days. I have a little saying which helps with this: 'All the way up and all the way down!' I say this every time they pull their pants up and down as it makes it a little bit more fun.

Ask your little trainer to show you where their potty/trainer seat is and get them sitting on it. If they refuse, try to distract them by asking them about the stickers or stars they're going to get or grab a book to read to them. More often than not, if you have distracted your toddler they will not even realise they are sitting on the potty/toilet. If they sit on the potty/toilet give them lots of praise: 'What a big boy/girl you are!' and let them choose a magic sticker or star. Half the battle at the beginning is getting little ones to sit on the potty/toilet so it's important that they are rewarded for this – they will then associate sitting on the potty/toilet as a positive thing. Once your little one has sat on the potty/toilet, take them to wash their hands so that they get into a good routine with hygiene.

## Signs your toddler needs a wee

When you start potty training, it's all eyes on your little trainer so you can recognise when they need a wee. Most little ones tend to do the same action each time but it will be different for each toddler. You will soon catch on as to which is your child's tell-tale sign:

**The wee dance** is common but by this time they really need to go, so be quick with the potty! It's normally a quick dance around the room or a bit of hopping about.

**Leg crossing** is also a sign that they need to go soon. It would be a good idea to get them to a potty/toilet quickly as crossing of the legs indicates they are trying to stop a wee coming out.

**Holding their pants** or pulling their pants is an indication that a wee is on its way out, so don't waste any time!

**Swaying from side to side,** becoming fidgety, and moving from one foot to the other is also an indication that they need to go.

## Signs your toddler needs a poo

**Wind.** Often your little trainer will pass wind and, although not so pleasant, this can be an indication that they need a poo or one is shortly on its way. Try not to make a thing out of the wind as you don't want to put your toddler off or embarrass them.

**Hiding.** So many little ones love to sneak off and hide or tuck themselves behind the sofa when they need a poo. Keep your eyes peeled if you have a little hider – you may blink and they will be gone, returning with an unwelcome present!

**Going quiet.** Another indication that a poo is on its way is that toddlers can go from playing and making lots of noise to becoming completely silent.

**Facial expressions.** This is an obvious one. Some little faces will go red. Some toddlers will screw their faces up. Some little ones will do both and add moans and groans, but either way you will be aware when it happens. Hopefully it won't be too late!

**Holding their tummy.** Little ones can also hold on to their tummy or say that their tummy hurts when they need a poo. It can take them a while to associate this tummy pain with needing a poo, but be patient as it will sink in eventually.

Ask your little one every 20–30 minutes whether they need to use the potty/toilet to do a wee or poo. Some little ones will eventually do a wee. This is a confidence-building day so you need to be patient. Watch for key signs that they need a wee, like swaying from side to side or grabbing on to their pants (see page 61). If they need a poo you will often smell something prior to the poo actually arriving or they will hide somewhere. Their facial expressions will also say it all! When you spot any signs that your little one needs a wee or poo (see page 62), try to quickly sit them on the potty/toilet.

Keep reminding your little one about the magic reward stars/stickers throughout the day. This really does give them encouragement and a reason to sit on the potty/toilet, but as it is only Day One, they might not remember, so use gentle prompts like, 'Wow! You have big boy/girl pants on today. Mummy/Daddy is so proud!' This acts as a gentle reminder that they are not wearing a nappy/pull-up.

Expect accidents today. It's still early in the process and lots of accidents on the first day are very normal. If a wee accident happens, say to your child: 'Never mind. Next time let's try and do a wee in the potty because you are such a big boy/girl.' Just explain to your little trainer that wees should go in the potty/toilet, not on the floor. If a poo accident happens, take the poo in the pants to the potty/toilet with your little one and show them that it goes in there.

When accidents happen it's important to be calm and reassuring and try not to get frustrated. A frustrated parent will not help! Calmly explain to your little trainer that it is not where the wee/poo goes and ask them where they think it goes. Try saying to your child: 'Never mind. Let's try again. Let's go and get some new big boy/girl pants.'

## Should boys stand or sit when weeing?

This is a common question that I get asked and it always amuses me to see that the children of parents who are pro-standing always revert back to sitting. I always train boys to sit while they are weeing as, initially, they do not have much control when standing and it can make them very distressed when they wee everywhere. Boys also tend to empty their bladder a lot more when they are sitting down. Asking a boy to stand while weeing is just another thing for them to think about during the early stages of potty training as they have to hold their penis and aim in the correct place. You will find that this comes naturally as they get a little bit older, though maybe not for some! It is also good for boys to sit as they have to do this when they poo, so it helps with consistency during training. My answer to this one is definitely to encourage boys to sit in the early stages.

Once your little one does their first wee in the potty, give them a lot of praise and a clap and say to them, 'Wow, look what you have done. This has made Mummy/Daddy very happy!' Get your little trainer to choose their magic reward sticker/star and, once this is done, empty the potty into the toilet and show them where the wee goes, waving 'bye-bye' to it. Make sure they wash and dry their hands.

When your little one does their first poo in the potty, again give them lots of praise – 'What a big boy/girl you are! You have done a poo. You are so clever and Mummy/Daddy is so proud' – and don't forget the three stars for their reward box or two stickers for their chart. This is such a great step for your little one as poos can take a bit longer to master.

When you are coming to the end of the day, count the rewards your little trainer has received together and let them know you are very excited to see how many stars/stickers they will get tomorrow. Say 'Wow! You are so special! Look how many magic stars/stickers you got today. What a good boy/girl you have been!' If they haven't managed to achieve any stars/stickers, make sure you still praise them for trying and explain that 'Tomorrow we can try even harder to get some stars/stickers.'

Just before you put your little one to bed, get them into the routine of sitting on their potty/toilet and only put their nappy/pull-up on just before they get into bed, making sure this is done in their bedroom. This means they will associate having their nappy/pull-up back on with bedtime.

If your little one still has a daytime nap, encourage them to sit on the potty/toilet again before you take them up to their bedroom and put their nappy/pull-up on. Once they wake up make sure they put their nappy/pull-up in the bin and put their big boy/girl pants back on. (Give their bottom a good wipe and ensure that they are clean and dry before they put on their big boy/girl pants and leave the bedroom.)

Make sure they have plenty of fluid throughout the day as this will keep their bladder and bowel working.

Read the potty training story to your little trainer at bedtime.

### A little word for the grown-ups

You have started your journey and a few accidents may have happened, but rest assured that this is totally normal. You may have a few wet pants to wash, but well done for getting through Day One. Tomorrow must be kept exactly like today, sticking to the same routine and keeping it consistent with nothing but positive thoughts, so don't give up – together we can do this!

# Day Two

As you did yesterday, once your little trainer wakes up get them to put their nappy/pull-up in the bin. I find this makes toddlers feel important and helpful but what you are teaching them is that their nappy/pull-up is not needed past the bedroom. Make sure you give your little one's bottom a good wipe and ensure that they are clean and dry before they put on their big boy/girl pants.

This morning would be a good time to sit and talk to your little one and find out how they are feeling about potty training. Let them know how well they have done and show them how many magic stars/stickers they have achieved so far and, if you are using the magic reward box, how many more stars they need to get in order to achieve their magical prize. It is really important every morning that you have this chat with your toddler and reflect on what they have achieved so far. They will start to have an understanding of their reward system which will help the routine sink into their minds and keep them motivated.

Keep to the same routine as Day One today. It is key that you ask your little trainer 'Where is your potty/

toilet?' and get them to show you as this is all part of the independence we are trying to encourage. Ask your child to remind you what they do in the potty/toilet and get them to sit on their potty/trainer seat before breakfast. A little distraction, such as a toy or singing a nursery rhyme, may be needed here just to get them to stay sitting for long enough.

Today is the day to introduce the flashcards (see page 45). Sit somewhere where your little one won't be distracted and look through the flashcards together. Hold up one at a time and get them to tell you what the picture is. This is a fun game for your little trainer to play with you, and it teaches them what potty training is all about through pictures and words, making it easier for them to grasp the essentials. This is why flashcards are such an important part of my programme. It is very easy for us to give commands to our children, but seeing our expectations visually gives them such a better understanding – the flashcards actually show them that wee and poo go in the potty/toilet. In addition, just seeing a picture of a little boy/girl sitting on the potty/toilet is hugely effective.

Once again, make sure your little trainer drinks plenty of fluid throughout the day as this will keep their bladder and bowel healthy and working, and thus avoid constipation.

If your little one is having lots of accidents today, please stick to pants and do not be tempted to put a nappy/pull-up back on as this will send your child mixed messages and undo everything you have achieved so far. I understand that lots of accidents can be very frustrating and it would be easy for you to feel as if your efforts are getting you nowhere, but please persevere as I know you will get there in the end. It would be good to have a carpet cleaning spray and a cloth to hand, just in case there are any accidents. I recommend you use a white cloth as I once made the mistake of using a coloured cloth and the colour came out and stained my carpet!

If your little one does have an accident just say, 'Oh dear, wee doesn't go there – it goes in the potty/toilet. Tell me, where does it go?' I always like to get toddlers to repeat back what I have told them so that the message is made very clear. Get your little trainer to pick fresh pants and say, 'No magic star/sticker this time. Let's try to get a magic star/sticker next time.' Using prompts through-out the day can really help, such as 'Don't forget to ask Mummy/Daddy for a wee/poo as it makes me so happy.'

As a reminder halfway through the day, count the magic stars/stickers with your little trainer to see how many they have. This will encourage them to try to achieve more in the afternoon. Don't forget the 'Big Count' at the end of the day and also let your little trainer know again how proud you are that they are now wearing big boy/girl pants. Even if you feel you haven't had a very successful day it's really important you still say to them, 'Well done for trying today.'

At bedtime, you can either read your little trainer a potty training story or talk to them about what they have achieved throughout the day.

## Language to use when potty training

It is key to remember to use simple but effective language when rewarding and praising your little trainer, such as: 'Well done. You have done a wee/poo – this makes me so happy. You are such a big boy/girl.' I am told so many times by parents 'I can't help but get cross when they have had an accident.' This is just our natural emotions coming to the fore, but the best way to deal with accidents is to say, 'I feel so sad you did this. Where does your wee/poo go?' It can be very easy to get impatient and angry when dealing with this situation but you must try your hardest not to show this. Take a few deep breaths in a different room if you need to.

Children relate better to expression than raised voices, and it is important that they do not associate potty training with anger as this could lead to a fear of potty training. Showing your emotions on your face is an effective way of communicating your feelings to your toddler and is a softer approach than getting angry or shouting. Toddlers learn very quickly the difference between a happy face and a sad face. Toddlers like to please, so if they see a happy face they will react well as they can see you are pleased with what they are doing. Sad faces show disappointment which is a gentle way of showing your toddler that what they did was wrong. I find that it helps to speak to little trainers like they are mini adults – it is okay to say in a firm but non-aggressive manner 'Poo or wee does not go in your pants or on the floor. Where does it go?'. Simply by pointing out to your toddler when they have had an accident and explaining to them where the wee/poo should go helps to give them a clearer under-standing of your expectations.

At this stage some little trainers can become very distressed and tearful when they have had an accident. If your child seems upset, comfort them and just gently explain that 'Accidents sometimes happen, so let's try to get the wee/poo in the potty/toilet next time.' It's never nice to see little ones get upset and we do not want to encour-age the association of fear with potty training as this will only have an overall negative impact on potty training.

Below are some words and key phrases I use in differ-ent situations during potty training:

## Prompts to sit or ask for the potty/toilet

- 'Don't forget to ask Mummy/Daddy for a wee as that makes me so happy.'

- 'Is it time for a wee or poo yet?'
- 'We are so excited to see you sit on the potty/toilet.'
- 'Wow, you look so special in your big boy/girl pants!'
- 'Mummy/Daddy cannot wait for you to get another magic star/sticker.'
- 'Is that a poo I can hear coming? Must be time to sit on the potty/toilet.'
- 'What a big boy/girl you are now you have your own special potty.'
- 'Is your potty magic? Shall we sit on it and see what happens?'

## When they have tried

- 'Next time let's try to do a wee/poo in the potty/toilet because you are such a clever boy/girl.'
- 'Never mind. Shall we try again next time you need a wee/poo?'
- 'Oh dear. Poo doesn't go in your pants. Shall we put the poo in the potty/toilet where it belongs?'
- 'Thank you so much for trying. You are such a good boy/girl.'
- 'Well done for trying. That has made Mummy/Daddy so happy.'
- 'I think I will give you a magic star/sticker for trying so hard today.'
- 'What a superstar you are today for trying.'
- 'We are so proud that you tried all by yourself.'

# When they have done a wee or poo in the potty

- 'Well done. You are such a big boy/girl.'
- 'Mummy/Daddy is so proud of you.'
- 'You did it! You are our winner!'
- 'Wow, you are so special. Mummy/Daddy loves you so much.'
- 'What a clever boy/girl you are. So amazing, you have done a wee/poo!'
- 'Hip hip hooray! You did a wee/poo!'
- 'You have so many magic stars/stickers. You are so clever.'
- 'You have been super special today.'
- 'I knew you were such a clever boy/girl.'
- 'You've done it all by yourself. What a clever boy/girl.'
- 'Let's wave bye-bye to the wee/poo.' (When flushing the toilet or tipping from the potty into the toilet.)

If, at any point you feel cross and frustrated, just take yourself off into another room and release your frustration away from your little trainer. When they are in bed, reward yourself with a large glass of something special!

**Q**: My three-year-old son has been potty trained for around six months now and fully understands the sensation of going to the toilet. He often asks me (Daddy) or Mummy when he needs to go at home, though sometimes we have to gently encourage him when he looks like he is holding it in. The problem we have now is that he is refusing to tell his child-minder when he needs to go to the toilet and, when she asks him, he says no. He then proceeds to have an accident in his pants – although it is not really an accident as he is fully aware he is doing it.

The childminder seems to react to this with a serious tone as she wants to convey to my son the 'severity' of what he is doing, but in my view her reaction borders on frustration and annoy-ance. I feel that the reaction is fuelling the problem and believe she should speak to my son calmly. The childminder refuses to take this calm, friendly tone as she believes that we need to make my son aware of the severity of the issue and she is trying to convey a consequence of disappointment and frustration.

**A**: I am afraid I totally disagree with your childminder. If you start introducing severity at this stage your son will associate potty training with something that upsets or annoys Mummy, Daddy or the childminder. I am a total believer in making potty training a fun and magical experience and what needs to happen here is to introduce some fun back into the situation. Your childminder's approach does concern me as it seems to me that your son is uncomfortable asking her when he needs to go to the toilet and this is becoming a habit or even a game to him. I would introduce a special reward system over the weekend that you and your wife can work on with your son and continue this while he is with the childminder. What is needed here is to turn all of this into a positive experience as soon as possible with the support of the childminder.

## A little word for the grown-ups

If today you feel it has been nothing but accidents and you are wondering whether your little one is actually ready, try to remember that this is completely normal and all part of the training process. It does take time for little ones' brains and bladders to connect, but rest assured that this will all happen in time. Remember, you have to be patient at this stage, even though you feel like pulling your hair out. It's only Day Two. Little ones can get very frustrated with themselves, and you at times, so please remember to be subtly persistent but back off if they become anxious.

# Day Three

As per the previous two days, once your little trainer wakes up, get them to put their nappy/pull-up in the bin and clean their bottom before letting them choose their big boy/girl pants.

By this stage your little trainer should have got the gist of their reward system and started to understand the routine. If accidents happen, keep an eye out for any pattern that is forming. Accidents can occur when they are busy playing, after lunch, or if you have a house full of visitors, so more prompts may be needed such as 'Don't forget to ask Mummy/Daddy if you need a wee' or 'Remember you have big boy/girl pants on.'

Sometimes the novelty of sitting on the potty/toilet may start to wear off at this stage, so this is a good time to use distraction with an object or game, or even start singing your child's favourite nursery rhyme with them while they are sitting on the potty/toilet. My programme is all about keeping potty training fun and keeping your little one interested. Most of the time children do not want to sit on the potty/toilet because they have better things to do, such as playing. They may not want to stop what they are doing, but it is down to you to take control of this, otherwise accidents will happen. Gently prompt your little one by saying, 'Wow, you are so special in your big boy/girl pants.' This can help to encourage them to ask rather than you constantly going on at them as endless questioning can make little ones very frustrated.

Keep an eye on your little one's bowel movements throughout this week because if they haven't been for a few days this can put pressure on the bladder and cause accidents. Make sure they are having enough fluid and fibre daily. Some exercise also helps to get their bowels moving. If you are concerned your little one may be constipated, see Chapter 7 for advice and speak to your doctor.

## Getting out and about

I am a great believer in getting out and about while potty training as we need to train toddlers to be dry inside and outside of the home. Today would be a good day to try this if you feel confident enough. Just go somewhere local – don't embark on any big journeys; maybe just try the local park for a short time. Get your toddler to sit on the potty/ toilet for at least five minutes before you venture out. I find that saying something like, 'Come on, let's do this wee so we can go out and have lots of fun!' really helps.

We all know public toilets are not the best or the most hygienic. As adults we don't like using them and every child I have potty trained at the beginning definitely has a dislike of using them, mainly because of the smell. So it's important to make sure you take your child's potty/trainer seat with you to keep the programme consistent and to avoid having to use unclean public toilet seats. You'll also need to pack spare pants and clothes including tissues or biodegradable wipes so that you have everything to hand

and are fully prepared in case an accident does occur. We do not want your toddler to associate going out and potty training as a stressful occasion.

While you are out and about make sure you still regularly remind your little one to sit on the potty/trainer seat as outside distractions may lead to an accident. They may be overexcited and having far too much fun that they forget to ask! Take two clear sandwich bags with you – one for transporting the magic stars/stickers and one for the magic stars/stickers to be put into once your little one has earned them. This will keep the rewards consistent and, once you get back home, your little trainer can put the stickers on their chart or the stars in their magic reward box.

**Q:** I look after my granddaughter who is 28 months old and has recently potty trained. She is completely dry inside the house, but seems to be having accidents only when we are out and about. Should I put her back into pull-ups when we venture out?

**A:** It's really great that your granddaughter is dry in the house. However, you can't stay inside all the time just because she is having accidents while out and about. She has obviously grasped the concept of potty training as she is having no accidents while at home, so this suggests to me that she is distracted and forgets to ask when she is outside the home. The first obvious step is making sure that she sits on the potty/toilet for 5–10 minutes before you leave home. I would also suggest that you take her potty/trainer seat out with you when you leave the home and make sure your granddaughter is aware that you have this. Gently remind her that if she needs to go for a wee then she must ask you as you have her potty/trainer seat. I would also create a reward system so that, if she stays dry when outside the home, she will get a reward of your choice. This will help to further encourage her.

## A little word for the grown-ups

I know what you are thinking: how on earth are we going to go out and about? I know it seems daunting, but if you do not do this after a few days you will find it a lot more difficult to train your little one outside the home. After all, you are probably going stir-crazy by now, and a bit of fresh air and some different scenery will be good for you both, so please do give it a try.

# Day Four

Don't forget, once your little trainer wakes up get them to put their nappy/pull-up in the bin, wipe them clean and let them choose their big boy/girl pants.

We are now at Day Four and you might have noticed that your little trainer is sitting on the potty/toilet on their own without you asking them to. If they are, this is an amazing achievement! At this stage, rather than asking your little trainer if they need the potty/toilet, I would like them to independently ask you when they need to go. If they are not already doing so, use more prompts by encouraging and reminding your toddler to use the potty/toilet rather than asking them outright. Say to them, 'Don't forget to ask Mummy/Daddy if you need a wee or poo as that makes me so happy.'

It is still early days, so stick to the routine and reward system. If you are using the magic reward box, by this time your little one should have nearly gained enough magic stars for their big prize. A gentle reminder of this should be enough to keep the excitement going. You could say to them, 'Wow! Look at all the magic stars you have. You only need two more to get the BIG prize!'

By Day Four, a lot of little trainers have got the general gist of potty training, but some may take a little longer. Keep repeating the programme and remember not to get frustrated. Lay out the flashcards and get your little one to shout out the answers. I like to mix things up a bit and change the answers – for example, holding up a flashcard with a poo on it and asking the toddler if it's a wee. Toddlers love this game and shouting out the correct answers really does make them feel special. Flashcards are also a good way of continuing the prompts using pictures. I often pick one out showing a wee or poo and say 'Do you need one of these?'

It is a good idea to venture outside again today as it builds your little trainer's confidence in leaving the home in their big boy/girl pants, but do ensure they sit on the potty/toilet before you leave the house. It's good to let your little one take their time so try not to rush them on the potty/toilet just so you can get out of the door quickly. You may need to use a distraction to keep them sitting a little longer.

Accidents may still happen and many little ones I have trained can have a really good run of being dry then suddenly have an accident at this stage. Most of the time it's because they are distracted by watching something on the TV or playing, so gentle reminders to ask you if they need to use the potty/toilet still need to be implemented throughout the day. It's not necessary to be as persistent as the last three days as some little ones can become very frustrated with you constantly asking – they can begin to shut down and not ask you at all – so try not to overdo it.

Be aware if you are having visitors or a play date today. The distraction of visitors can easily cause your little one to forget to ask for the potty/toilet so more prompts may be needed from you. Little ones get very excited and can forget if they need to go, so keep an eye out for the wee dance, holding their pants or crossing their legs (see page 61). If you have visitors, some little ones are very shy about sitting on the potty in front of them so you may need to reposition their potty in a more discreet place. Keep your eyes peeled and, if you think your little one needs to go, go over to them and gently ask them if they need the potty/toilet. Make a point of getting your toddler to show your visitors their magic stars/stickers as this will give them a great sense of pride and encouragement.

Do not forget to do the 'Big Count' at the end of the day. A phone call to grandparents or other family members with your little one telling them how many magic stars/stickers they have today will also really help. This not only pleases your little trainer but it will brighten up any grandparent's day!

## A little word for the grown-ups

As with any new milestone in your little one's life, it is always special to share the achievement with family and friends. Getting all your loved ones involved in potty training is very special for your little trainer and for you as a parent to share your success.

# Day Five

I am sure you have got it by now – nappy/pull-up in the bin, a wipe clean, and then let your little trainer choose their big boy/girl pants.

So, we have finally reached Day Five! I am sure you have been through some challenging days this week, but rest assured that this is completely normal – potty training is not an easy task for most of us parents or the little trainers involved. However, once your little one has got the hang of it, it is a great new stage in their development – for your little trainer to suddenly have to remember and ask when they need to go to the potty/toilet instead of just doing it in their nappy/pull-up like they have done for the last two years or so is pretty impressive. It is incredible how much little toddlers can learn over just a few days if using the correct tools. I always think of them as little sponges, because they soak everything up.

Hopefully by now your little one is coming to you to ask to use the potty/toilet and, if they are, this is amazing! If this is not the case, start using more prompts throughout the day, such as, 'You look so special in your big boy/girl pants' or 'We are so excited to see you sit on the potty/toilet' – you really need to encourage them to ask and not be told.

Every child is different and some may just need a little bit more time. Over the many years of working with toddlers, the key thing to achieving successful results is consistency from Day One and continuing with the programme until you have achieved what you set out to do. Keep the continuity of reward and praise for a few more weeks depending on your child's progress. This will keep your little one engaged and, most of all, make potty training enjoyable and fun. Some parents I have worked with have stopped the rewards too soon and have then seen reoccurring accidents. You have worked so hard together that a little longer will not hurt. Do not forget to keep reminding your toddler and pointing out that the sticker chart/magic reward box is waiting for stickers/stars and maybe nudge them now and again – 'How do you get a sticker/star?' – as busy little trainers have lots of playing to do during the day and may forget.

At this stage, some little ones will have mastered potty training during the day but, even if you think your toddler has got the hang of things, I urge and encourage you to continue my fun and magic programme until you are completely satisfied that your little one is having no or very few accidents. Stopping the continuity too soon may lead to them regressing.

Here are some key things to remember over the next few weeks:

- Let your child take their nappy/pull-up off when they wake up and put it in the bin.
- Wipe them clean and then let them choose their big boy/girl pants.
- Get them to take you to their potty/trainer seat and encourage them to sit on it.
- Encourage your toddler to ask you when they need to go rather than you telling them.
- Keep rewarding their successes.
- Ensure your child is washing their hands properly.
- Give them a healthy, balanced diet and offer plenty of fluid throughout the day.
- Keep your child's childcare setting up to date with progress.
- Take your child's potty/trainer seat out wherever you go.
- Keep the rewards going when out and about.
- Ensure you have spare clothes and plenty of pants with you when you're outside the house, just in case.

You have reached the end of the week and I know this will have been as big a step for you as a parent as it has been for your little one. You did it! I know how patient you will have been and I am sure the washing machine will have been on constantly. You deserve a big reward yourself for moving your toddler on to their next stage.

You may still see some accidents as the days go on, but try prompting and encouraging your toddler to ask you to use the potty/toilet rather than telling them to go. If you feel they still haven't got into a routine with potty training then just keep repeating the programme until they have. I am not expecting your little one to be 100 per cent trained by Day Five, but I'm hoping they are beginning to be well on their way.

# 5 Moving Forward

I t's great that you have reached this stage with your little one! Now it's time to move forward with their final bit of training.

## Transitioning from Potty to Trainer Seat

O nce your little one has mastered using the potty for a few weeks with no accidents, start moving the potty next to the toilet you want them to use in the house. Remember to make sure your little one helps you with this process as, again, getting them involved is key.

It's important to make sure the bathroom is inviting for your little one with a fun hand soap and a little basket of books and toys – a favourite trick of mine is to take turns blowing bubbles to keep them occupied! This will help to distract your toddler and get them to sit on the toilet for longer periods. And don't forget the step stool to help your little one to reach the toilet and sink, but also ensure they are correctly positioned when sitting on the toilet (see page 39).

Transitioning to the big toilet is another important stage in your child's development, but it can sometimes be a little tricky so, again, it's about making light of it and, most of all, making it fun for your little one. When I help with the transition from potty to trainer seat I always explain to the child, 'Now that you are such a big girl/boy you can go into the big bathroom like Mummy/Daddy.' To help make life easier for you, try to buy a trainer seat in the same colour/design as your child's potty in preparation for this transition. This means it's not such a huge change for your little one to adjust to and it keeps the continuity going.

**Q**: My youngest son has a fear of falling into the toilet. I never used a trainer seat with my other four children. Is it really necessary?

**A**: It can be very daunting for little ones when they move on to the big toilet from a potty – most toilet seats are far too big for little bottoms and it's very hard for toddlers to get a good balance, so it's not uncommon for children to be frightened of falling in. I'm a big fan of trainer seats for this transition period as they create a smaller area and a far more comfortable seat that will not make toddlers feel like they are going to drop through.

If your son seems a little wary of using the toilet, it's a good idea to use a trainer seat to enable him to sit properly and feel secure. If he is not relaxed when he is sat on the toilet it is going to set him back. If your little one still wants to use the potty, you can place the trainer seat on the toilet anyway and, if they choose to try both, just go with it. More often than not toddlers will gravitate towards the trainer seat after a few weeks. Keep the encouragement going by continuing to use the magic rewards/stickers for this transition.

Most little ones will use a trainer seat for a few months. It will be down to you to judge when they are ready to transition from the trainer seat to the toilet seat itself, but there is no rush. Most little ones will prompt you themselves when they are ready without too much fuss.

Some little ones are afraid of the toilet flushing as they feel they are going to get sucked into it. I always show my little trainers suffering with this fear a little piece of toilet paper thrown down the toilet. Get them to flush it and this generally stops the fear after a few attempts. If this is not the case for your child, then to avoid training regression, just flush the toilet once they have left the bathroom.

## A little word for the grown-ups

When this transition is taking place, some little ones will have a fear of the toilet, so continue to do your best to make it feel safe and fun for them. Rewards can be continued until your little trainer gets used to the idea. Bathrooms are a place we should all feel relaxed in to take our time when doing our business. Some adults choose to read papers to relax and little ones are no different. Make sure you exercise patience so your toddler is completely chilled and don't rush them when they are sat on the toilet as they are probably not in any hurry!

# Night-Time Training

'How or when do I start night-time potty training?' This is the all-time big question I get asked by parents. As for daytime training, before you start you need to look for signs your toddler is ready (see page 91). I tell the parents I work with to make sure their child is completely dry in the day for at least a couple of months before even attempting night-time training. It's so important not to push night-time training too early. Children can be up to four or five years old before they are completely dry at night as night-time dryness involves different bladder control than during the day. Some children sleep deeper than others, which means that they are not aware when they have a full bladder which can lead to bed-wetting (see page 102).

## Signs of readiness

When your little one has mastered daytime potty training, has been dry for at least a couple of months and you start noticing a pattern where they wake up in the morning with a dry nappy/pull-up, this is a good sign that they are ready to take their night-time nappy/pull-up off. Another sign is if your little one decides that they don't want to wear their nappy/pull-up and, in the middle of the night, takes it off themselves! They may also start waking you up asking to use the potty/toilet during the night. Try to avoid putting a nappy/pull-up on your child once you start night-time training as they won't then worry if they wet it as they feel they have protection.

## Be prepared

Being prepared is key, so here are a few items you will need before you start night-time training:

# Night light

Young children are often scared of the dark, so invest in a good night light which gives off a soft glow for the hallway and their bedroom. This will help guide them to the potty/toilet without feeling daunted by getting up in the dark.

# Waterproof mattress protector

Always be on the safe side is something I would say with night-time training. Mattress protectors are not very expensive and are widely available. The last thing you and your little trainer need is a soaking wet mattress in the middle of the night, which will be very distressing for all of you and will eventually damage and stain your mattress.

# Spare sheets

It is always good to have a few spare sheets so, if your little one does have an accident, you can quickly change the bed without any stress. It's a good idea to keep your sheets in a handy place so you can do a quick changeover because, believe me, in the middle of the night everything seems a lot worse and it's really important for your toddler that this is a quick change around and a big issue is not made of it.

## Get started

Before you start night-time potty training, it's really important that you sit down and explain to your little trainer that they will not have a nappy/pull-up on when they go to bed, and if they need a wee or poo they must go on the potty/toilet. Make sure you put a potty in their bedroom, near a night light if possible, and make them aware of where it is. If they are using a trainer seat, make sure they have a soft light in the bathroom to help guide them to it in the dark. Loose pyjamas or nighties are a must – no all-in-ones or drawstring pyjama bottoms as your little one won't have time to master these when they are sleepy as well as finding the potty/toilet.

Ensure you have a good bedtime routine. Make sure you reduce fluids at least 30 minutes before bedtime – this includes fruit as some fruit, such as watermelon, straw-berries, pineapple, oranges, raspberries and cucumber, contain up to 80 per cent water. Get your little trainer to sit on the potty/toilet before bedtime so that they fully empty their bladder. It may take a little bit of distracting to keep them on there that little bit longer – try reading them a book or blowing bubbles – but it's important to encour-age your toddler to sit there for at least 3–5 minutes.

It is important that your toddler is not constipated when you choose to start night-time training as their bowel will be very full and this can put extra pressure on their bladder which can lead to bed-wetting. If you are concerned your little one may be constipated, see Chapter 7 for advice and speak to your doctor.

**Q**: My little one has been potty trained during the day for a few weeks with the odd accident. Shall I start night-time potty training with her?

**A**: Night-time training is very different to the day because your child is asleep. Your little one has only just mastered daytime training so I would advise you to wait a few more weeks. Look out for the key signs that she is ready for night-time potty training (see page 91). When your daughter wakes up for at least a week or two with a dry nappy, this is a good sign she is ready. When she is showing signs she is ready make sure you are prepared: buy a mattress protector, a night light and some spare sheets (just in case), and start reducing liquids at least 30 minutes before her bedtime.

## Rewards

I love rewarding toddlers throughout any milestone because I think it is important we recognise when they do things right, and night-time training is another huge thing to tick off the list.

Once your toddler wakes up dry in the morning, make sure you give them lots of praise: 'Well done – you are such a big girl/boy! We are so happy.' You can then reward them with a sticker/star as before and they can achieve a special prize at the end of the week. A reward system can also be used to encourage them to make sure they sit on the potty/toilet before bed.

## School Readiness

Another stage in your child's development is complete, and your toddler is turning into an independent little person – from feeding themselves, walking, talking and dressing, to finally being potty trained. All of a sudden, it is time for them to go to school! As a parent I found this stage very difficult – I didn't feel my little babies were ready and the thought of being separated from them all day really upset me. How would they cope without me? How would they dress themselves properly? Would they remember to go to the toilet and wash their hands? There were so many things to think about and, being protective as a parent, I sent myself into overdrive. Having been through this huge milestone with all three of my children, and working professionally with many other families, the best advice I can give you is to get your little one prepared as much as you can.

Once you know which school your little one is going to, you will be offered a school visit together. Try to get the most out of these visits – I always looked round every part of the school so I had a good understanding of how the school worked and, of course, I checked out the toilets!

You have already had a good start with hygiene while you were potty training your child and teaching them to go to the toilet independently. Throughout this book I have emphasised the importance of teaching our little ones good hygiene as soon as they are able to understand. Keep instilling this message and ensure they are washing their hands properly. Lots of children start their Reception year unable to wipe their bottoms properly, so it's important that you pay special attention to this in the run up to your child starting school. It can make them uncomfortable and fidgety if their bottom is not wiped properly. If you have any concerns whatsoever about your little one asking to go to the toilet please speak to the teacher prior to them starting. Sometimes there can be the odd accident at the start of Reception, but primary school teachers are very used to this, so do not think your child is an isolated case. Often children who have just started school have accidents because they are in new surroundings, there is a change in their routine or they are just too afraid to ask. Pop some spare clothes in your child's school bag in case of accidents (and don't forget to label them!).

**Q**: My son has just started pre-Reception at a public school and, because he is having so many accidents still, one might say that he isn't fully potty trained. Understandably, the teacher and teaching assistant cannot cater for our son throughout the day and take care of the rest of the students – that is not fair on anyone. We are taking it day-by-day and have our third day at school tomorrow, but we are already having talks with the teacher about how we may need to pull him out until he is fully toilet trained. The school and his ex-nursery seem to agree that he knows what to do and is consciously choosing not to go. We have tried so many different methods, but it has now got to the stage where he is showing no interest in using the potty and in recent weeks does not seem bothered by it all. Please help!

**A**: I want to reassure you that this is not an isolated case. Starting school can sometimes have a huge impact on a child and, more often than not, the way they deal with this is by holding on when they need to go to the toilet or begin to have accidents. At this stage I would advise to take some time out from school for a week or two and implement a structured training programme at home, almost like starting all over again. Introduce a reward system that engages and excites your son, and make it clear what goals he has to achieve. Make this something he has to really work for and have a big prize at the end of each week.

## A little word for the grown-ups

Your little baby starting school can be a very emotional time for you as a parent. Every single time one of my children walked off into the new school on their first day, I walked away in floods of tears and not one of them looked back at me! I remember counting the minutes on their first day until it was time to go and pick them up and I arrived 30 minutes early! They absolutely loved their first day so I don't know what I was worrying about, plus the house was a lot tidier! This is a great milestone and the beginning of a new chapter for you all as a family, and you should feel proud of what you have achieved.

# 6 Potty Training Dilemmas

P otty training can go wrong for many different reasons, so try not to be disheartened if your
toddler encounters some issues along the way as
these can usually be easily rectified.

## Wee Dilemmas

W ees are normally the easy part of potty training. Yes,
you may have a few puddles at the beginning but
that is completely normal and to be expected. Damp pants
are also common and are often a result of your toddler not
wiping properly or not finishing or emptying their bladder

fully because they are in a hurry to get back to whatever they were doing before.

I'm a great believer in talking to children. It is useful and so important to talk with your toddler and ask them why they didn't make it to the potty/toilet in time. They may have no reason or explanation, but try to just listen to them and be calm and considerate in your response as the accident has probably upset them too. Reassure them and say something like, 'Never mind. What a silly wee. It didn't even tell you it was coming.'

If you notice that your toddler is having lots of accidents after they have been trained, this could be an indication that something else is going on. It will be nothing that can't be fixed, so don't panic. It's worth noting that constipation can put pressure on the bladder and cause accidents, and general illness can also set your toddler back. It's also important to rule out a urinary tract infection (see page 133).

## Emotional distractions

If a toddler becomes distressed or frustrated about something – and it doesn't have to be related to toilet training – it can overtake their lives and totally throw them off course and lead to accidents. This can be triggered by anything from being upset about an incident at nursery or a change in the household, such as moving house or a new baby, to simply being scared of the dark.

Any type of upset can really interfere with your toddler's routine and if they are worried about something it can have a huge impact on their progress. Try speaking to your little one to get to the bottom of whatever the problem is, and offer them the support they need to combat it. Then you can get back on track with the training again.

## Holding on to their wee

Another factor that can lead to accidents is your toddler holding on to their wee. Some little ones have a fear of potty training which can cause them to hold on to their wee, while others simply cannot be bothered to stop what they are doing to have a wee, which leads to them holding on to it. This can lead to so many problems as, when the bladder is not emptied regularly, bacteria can grow and multiply, which in turn can cause a UTI (urinary tract infection). It is important to ensure your little one drinks plenty of fluid as, if they do not, their brain may not be giving the message to their bladder to empty regularly enough.

## Deliberate accidents

Sometimes little ones will stand and deliberately have an accident just because they are being stubborn or are trying to gain your attention. In this instance I would recommend saying something like: 'This has made me sad. You know that's not what you do. Next time it needs to go in the potty or toilet.' It's really important to refrain from getting cross in situations like this. Keep your language simple and direct, but make sure you are clear in your message as it's key that your little one understands that what they have done is not acceptable.

## Bed-wetting

Bed-wetting can be common in little ones and usually there are no obvious reasons why children wet the bed. However, bed-wetting can really turn the household upside down at night for you as parents. It can be a tiring exercise changing the bedding in the middle of the night, and let's not forget the sleep deprivation that goes with it.

Many parents restrict their child's fluid intake during the day in a bid to stop them wetting the bed at night. However, it is so important that your toddler has plenty of fluid throughout the day and that they go on the potty/toilet regularly as it makes their bladder stronger at night.

So how can you reduce the risk of bed-wetting? My top tips include:

- Reducing liquids 30–60 minutes before bedtime.
- Making sure your little one uses the potty/toilet before

bedtime and sits on there for a good 5–10 minutes to ensure they fully empty their bladder (read them a story to distract them if necessary).

- Lighting the area where the potty/toilet is with a soft light as the majority of little ones are afraid of the dark.
- Using a reward system with stars and the magic reward box, but make a special bedtime star (this encourages them and gets them into a routine).

I always reward little ones for using the potty/toilet before bed rather than achieving a dry bed. Toddlers will not wet the bed deliberately, so it's important that you don't punish your little one for bed-wetting as this can make them feel nervous or afraid to go to bed.

## Should you lift?

Many parents 'lift' their little ones before they themselves go to bed to avoid bed-wetting. Lifting is when parents get their child out of bed and physically put them on the potty/toilet. However, there are mixed views on this. I have always been of the opinion that you should try everything else first before it gets to the stage where you feel you need to lift your child. I feel that your child should be aware of what is happening and, if they are half asleep, they will not know what is going on so this will not cure bed-wetting. However, after trying everything, if lifting works for you for a few weeks and that is what you choose to do, try to gently wake your child first so they are aware of what is going on.

## Some common causes

Some little ones are deep sleepers and their brain does not respond to signals from their bladder so they don't wake up when their bladder is full. This can be a sign that they are not fully ready yet in their development, so it would be better to hold off with night-time training for a month, and keep an eye on how wet or dry their nappies/pull-ups are in the mornings. If they start to seem dry then try again.

Bed-wetting can sometimes be linked to emotional situations. Your little one could be worried about a change like a new baby, starting nursery or moving house. This is more likely to be the case once they have been dry for long periods then suddenly start wetting the bed.

Fizzy drinks, tea, coffee and hot chocolate all contain caffeine and will lead to the bladder being overactive, so it's important to avoid giving these to your child.

Bed-wetting can also be linked to an underlying health issue such as constipation, if the bowel becomes full it can put extra pressure on the bladder which can lead to bed-wetting. Urinary tract infections can also cause bed-wetting so keep an eye out for signs of this (see page 133). If you're at all worried about your child's health, please consult your doctor.

## A little word for the grown-ups

Bed-wetting is a very common problem, not only in toddlers but in older children too. You would be very surprised by how many people experience this problem – half a million children in the UK alone have issues with bed-wetting. Bed-wetting can be just as tough on parents as it is on little ones, so please do not beat yourselves up about it as night-time training can take longer with some children. The best advice I can give you is to be prepared for night-time accidents with spare bedding close to hand. Patience, as always, is also key. If you are concerned about your child's bed-wetting you can get in touch with ERIC, The Children's Bowell and Bladder Charity (eric.org.uk).

# Poo Dilemmas

Poo has been the troublemaker for many of my little trainers over the years, whether it is holding the poo in, or hiding behind the sofa when doing a poo. My eldest daughter had a pleasant habit of handing me her poo while I was driving! I am sure many of you will have your own funny stories to tell on this journey.

I am a great believer in talking to toddlers and explaining to them what poo is in very simple terms – telling them: 'It has to come out of your tummy so you can eat more yummy food!' Try mentioning some of the foods that you know your little one loves.

Mastering poos can take extra time, for no other reason than some toddlers just refuse point-blank to do it on the potty/toilet, or they do not want to stop what they are doing and this leads to them holding it in. I often introduce extra rewards for pooing in the correct place as, in a toddler's eyes, it takes more effort so deserves special recognition.

I find that making potty training a bit of fun helps to relax toddlers and can turn many issues around. Over the years, I have devised several different tactics that children enjoy and respond well to, including:

- Making the bathroom a fun place and keeping it warm and inviting. Why not put their name on the door in sparkly paper? Try to avoid using strong-smelling products such as bleach, as smells like this can make the bathroom seem intimidating for little ones.
- Explaining that we all need to poo including mummies, daddies, pets and their favourite characters.

- Rewarding and praising your toddler to help encourage them, even if it is just for trying.

- Putting a basket of toys or books next to the potty/toilet ready to distract your little one. A favourite trick of mine is getting out the bubbles – taking turns blowing bubbles is the best distraction I have found, and always helps to relax toddlers for that bit longer.

- Being patient. Never get cross or angry with your toddler if they refuse to do a poo. It's likely that they already have a slight issue with poos so you need to try not to make it worse. Small steps to help encourage them, such as extra rewards for pooing, plenty of praise and patience, are needed instead. Use upbeat prompts such as 'Is it time for your poo yet?' or 'It makes Mummy/Daddy very happy when you do a poo.' This helps to reassure your little one that it is okay to poo.

## Pooing in pants

Often little ones will poo in their pants and come to you afterwards. At this stage it is important to try to teach your toddler where the poo should go. I take my little trainers and their soiled pants over to the potty/toilet and tip the poo into it. We wave bye-bye to the poo to make light of the situation. More often than not, toddlers are in denial that they even need a poo and so it's important to keep potty training upbeat in order to overcome this psychological barrier and encourage them to do a poo voluntarily.

Over the years I have found that using potty training flashcards relating to poo with my little trainers seems to relax them and give them a better understanding of what is expected. It's a good idea to give these a try with your little one if they are pooing in their pants (see page 45 for more on using flashcards).

## Withholding poo/refusing to go

Throughout my years of training countless toddlers, the most common problem parents face is their child withholding a poo or refusing to go. Both these issues generally stem from an overall fear of pooing. Usually this will have originated with the toddler having previously passed a hard poo which was uncomfortable and caused them some pain, which then led to a fear of them letting go. We must therefore try our best to avoid this becoming a problem, and find a way to relax littles ones and eliminate the fear. Toddlers can easily turn this fear into a habit, so the sooner we turn this around the better.

It is vital that you try to avoid constipation as, if your little one becomes constipated, their tummy will become uncomfortable and it will hurt when passing their poo, which can make them more reluctant to let go. Ensure that your little trainer drinks plenty of fluid during the day. Daily exercise is also key to keep everything moving and promote a healthy bowel. If you find your toddler is slightly constipated, a nice warm bath and a gentle rub on their tummy afterwards really help. (See pages 140–147 for more on constipation.)

Some little ones find going for a poo intimidating – the sounds, the smell or just the sheer embarrassment of going in front of parents or others puts them off – so try to be as discreet as possible. Don't make it a huge issue or put them centre stage. If you feel embarrassment is an issue for your toddler, place their potty in a discreet place where they feel comfortable.

During training, when you clearly see the warning signs that your toddler needs a poo – whether it is a smell or a particular facial expression – say 'I am going to leave the room now', as I have learnt over the years that, just as adults do not like to poo with an audience, little ones feel exactly the same way. A lot of the time toddlers will say that they do not need to go, but try walking away and saying 'Call me when your poo has arrived in the potty/toilet. I will be waiting outside the door with your magic stars/stickers as it is going to make me so happy when I see your poo has arrived.' It is all about finding what works with your little one, and using encouraging and fun techniques to let them know that it is okay to poo. Here are some practical tips I have used over the years:

## Explain

Toddlers are like sponges. I always sit down with my little trainers and explain to them what poo is in simple terms. Explain to your toddler that if they want to have some yummy food in their tummy then they need to do a poo so they can make some room. I find it helps to point out that we all do poos – mummies, daddies, teachers, dogs, cats (or whatever their pet is), even their favourite character – to encourage them. Ask your little one why they don't like poos. Try to find out what is bothering them so you can try to change this.

Over the many years I have been training toddlers and working with different families I have learnt that it's so important to come down to their level and find out what it is that makes them feel anxious about doing a poo. It is easy to just see it as them being stubborn and refusing to go, but it's not necessarily as simple as that in their eyes. Yes, toddlers do tend to have a little defiant streak in them at this age, but I have never felt that this is the case when it comes to doing a poo – it is more likely the fear of doing one. We have to work with our little ones in a calm and understanding way to enable them to overcome their anxious feeling of doing a poo in the potty/toilet.

## Use lots of rewards and praise

I like to make going for a poo as fun as possible as we don't want our little ones thinking of poo as an unhappy thing to do. Try giving your toddler extra rewards, stars or stickers and make a big deal of it if they go for a poo. Make sure you reward your toddler even if they just ask to do a poo – say to them, 'Well done for trying. You have made Mummy/Daddy very happy.' With many of my little trainers I have offered a sticker for their chart for asking to go for a poo, and a star for their magic reward box for actually doing a poo in the potty/toilet, just to make things a bit more special.

Little ones love to please their parents. Rewards and praise have a huge impact on their progress and it really does encourage them to try harder if they think they have pleased you.

## Let them take their time

When your little one says they need a poo, or you see the signs that they need one (see page 62), make sure you calmly try to encourage them to sit on the potty/toilet. Have objects close by the potty/toilet to distract them and make sure that they take their time. Try to relax your little one by pulling out one of their favourite books or toys. A favourite trick of mine is taking turns blowing bubbles – this is the best distraction I have found and I always keep bubbles with me just for this. Try saying to your child: 'Oh, is this a poo coming? Amazing. I think it's time to get the magic bubbles out. SO exciting!' Not only does blowing bubbles captivate most little ones, it really helps release the poos because the action of blowing helps relax the sphincter muscles.

## Will only poo with a nappy/pull-up on

Sometimes toddlers will only poo with a nappy/pull-up on. I have come across this issue with a few of my trainers over the years and have had to resort to putting a nappy/pull-up back on them, but for poos only. If this is something your little one does, it's important to avoid them holding on to their poo for long periods of time as this will make the poo hard and lead to constipation, which you definitely do not want! If your little one insists on having a nappy/pull-up on to poo then let them. However, as your ultimate goal is to try to achieve them sitting on the potty/toilet for a poo, make sure that, once they have done the poo, you remove the nappy/pull-up, take your little trainer and the soiled nappy/pull-up to the potty/toilet and tip the poo into it. It's essential that you show your toddler where the poo should go and speak to them using a friendly, warm tone. Wave 'bye-bye' to the poo and flush it away, making sure your toddler checks that it's gone. Try to make it a bit of fun by saying 'Poos like to go straight into the potty/toilet because they really like to get flushed all away!' Cheer together and have a big clap once you have flushed the poo away. This will help to reinforce to your toddler where their poo is meant to go. Make sure your toddler then puts their big boy/girl pants back on and washes their hands.

Gradually try moving your little one next to the potty/toilet when they are doing a poo in their nappy/pull-up and eventually you can try removing it when they have enough confidence. If they are still nervous about pooing you could always place the nappy/pull-up in the toilet bowl to 'catch' the poo and then tip the poo down the toilet as usual.

You will notice that most little trainers will have a favourite place that they like to go off to to do a poo, so place the potty in that place and walk away. Just say to them 'If you need the potty to catch your poo then it's just over there.' Continue with this until you feel your little one is confidently pooing independently. This could take time, so it is important to go at your child's pace and be patient.

# The Terrible Twos

The 'terrible twos' is a stage we all dread as parents and we wonder when it will be sprung upon us. My children all went through a very small stage of this, but luckily it did not last too long. However, it did leave me wondering why this happens: why is my once-perfect little baby now screaming and behaving like a little monster? And how on earth will I potty train them when they won't listen to anything I say?

It is so easy to judge other parents when we are out and about and there is a little person lying in the middle of the floor screaming and crying, but as soon as we become parents and these tantrums begin unexpectedly, we realise that this is not a case of bad parenting – it is toddlers showing signs of becoming defiant and reaching another stage in their development.

I think the term 'terrible twos' is a little harsh as this age can be such an amazing time. It's such a shame that parents dread this stage as little ones are super cute at this age and their little personalities really start to shine through – you can have some wonderful and highly amusing conversations with a two-year-old! This is also the age when most little ones start to show signs of independence.

A common concern I hear from parents is 'I want to start potty training because my little one is showing signs they are ready, but they are also refusing to do anything they are told!' You can't put off potty training simply because your little one is going through a phase, especially if they are indicating that they are ready. I always encourage parents to follow it through and just go with it. I honestly feel that potty training can help at this stage as it is encouraging your little one's independence. A lot of the time with two-year-olds, tantrums are a sign of frustration, and potty training is teaching them to recognise their body's signals and empowering them to go and do something for themselves. This can often deflect from other frustrations that they may have.

## Signs of the terrible twos

**Public screaming tantrums** – where your little one refuses to get off the floor in the middle of the supermarket – is the most common sign that they are going through this stage.

**Kicking and biting** is also common and can be something toddlers do to get their point across. It is not unusual for this to happen in a childcare setting with other children, or often Mummy or Daddy will get a kick or be bitten.

**The word 'NO'** is something toddlers will say at almost everything you ask them to do. They use this word to test parents and they tend to say it to anything. It could be the offer of a drink, asking them if they need the toilet or are hungry, asking them to pick up a toy, or a sign that they are getting frustrated because you have given them the wrong colour toy, plate or cup. This is very common. If you give your little one their food on a plate they didn't want or a cup that is the wrong colour, it can lead to huge frustration, which then results in them having a meltdown or even throwing the food off the plate.

## What to do

Public tantrums can be very embarrassing, but try not to worry about onlookers. Just concentrate on your little screamer. If you are in a public place, such as a supermarket or restaurant, and your little one kicks off, pick them up calmly, find a quiet spot and talk to them. If they are kicking and waving their arms and legs about just firmly wrap your arms around them until they calm down. Ask them, 'What's the matter? Why all these tears? Tell Mummy/Daddy what's wrong.' Just hug them and try to diffuse the situation. Do not start offering your toddler sweets or treats to distract them from the tantrum as this indicates a reward for their behaviour and will encourage them to behave like it again. Do not get angry with them either as this will only make the situation worse. I know it's hard in the heat of the moment, but try to stay calm. You can also try to distract your toddler by getting them to help find things in the supermarket as a little game. It is a great trick that nearly always worked for me!

Biting, kicking or hitting are not acceptable, and it is really important that you try to nip these behaviours in the bud as soon as you see they are about to take place. If you suspect your toddler is about to bite, kick or hit, then you must get down to their level, look them straight in the eye, hold their arms and say, 'No. We don't bite/kick/hit'. Make sure you keep looking your little one in the eye and repeat this message, but keep it simple. Just a firm 'No' is also okay. If they continue to try to do it, I recommend time out in another room for at least 10 minutes or sit them with you. This usually works as little ones do not like to miss out. The most important thing is to try to calm them down.

If your toddler starts shouting 'NO' at everything you offer them or ask them to do then you need to turn this around. Their seeming defiance can be because this is a word that we as parents tend to use a lot with our children! I always use the tactic of saying, 'No. What do you mean no?' Whatever you have asked them to do change it into a sentence of encouragement, so 'Are you hungry?' becomes 'Would you like some yummy food?'; 'Are you going to help Mummy/Daddy pick up that toy?' becomes 'That's very sad. It would make Mummy/Daddy very happy if you picked up that toy'; and 'Do you need a wee/poo?' becomes 'We would be so happy if you would try to sit on the potty/toilet.'

If you offer your toddler something that they clearly do not want and say 'No' to, it's very important to instil manners into them at this early age. Try 'Is that a "No thank you" I hear? That's better.' Make sure you praise them for being a good boy/girl as this will further encourage them.

Rejecting the wrong colour plate or cup and throwing the contents on the floor can be testing for even the most patient parent. Most babies before the age of two will do this unintentionally as they are still learning how to hold their food and control their plate or cup – this is part of them developing their fine motor skills. However, once they reach two years old it becomes more of an intentional action and your toddler will be doing this to get a reaction, to get attention, or just to be completely defiant! Just pick the plate back up and say 'Food doesn't go on the floor, it stays on the plate.' Do not put the plate back on your child's high chair or table. If you keep offering it back to them it will become a game and that plate will keep flying across the room. Once the plate is taken away your toddler will soon realise that this is not a game and you are certainly not willing to play it. When your toddler is eating nicely, use positive language such as 'You are such a good boy/girl eating your food nicely.' This will really encourage them as they are pleasing you and it will help promote that good behaviour which is essential when potty training.

I am a great believer that at mealtimes you should try to encourage the whole family to eat together. If your little one is in a high chair, make sure it is placed at the family table. This is something I did with all of my children. It inspires little ones to eat more and try different foods, and really encourages table manners with the additional lesson that mealtimes are not a game. It is also great for increasing family conversations so I am a huge fan of eating together, even if it is just for one meal a day.

One more quick tip is to make sure you remove the family dog from beneath the highchair or table! I'm sure your dog will not thank me for this as it will be missing out on the wonderful scraps your toddler loves to throw at it, but if this is allowed then it will quickly become a game and a huge distraction for your little one at mealtimes.

Most toddlers will display one or more of the above behaviours at some point, but my advice to you would be to find a way to not lose your temper or shout at them. This will only fuel what they are doing and will not get you the desired result. Try your best to stay calm using language that explains to your child in a simple way why they should not be behaving like this. Getting them to calm down is the most important thing as trying to explain anything to a toddler during a tantrum will only fall on deaf ears. Wait for your little one to calm down, sit with them and listen. Let them experiment with their independence: let them choose their plate or cup; let them help you make their lunch or dinner; let them put their trainer seat on the toilet; let them help you with picking items in the supermarket. I bought a toy trolley so my children could help me by putting some of the shopping into their trolley. They loved this and it seemed to deflect from any embarrassing supermarket tantrums.

Introducing your toddler to the idea of a routine – for example, by having regular distraction-free mealtimes – ensures your little one becomes familiar with consistency in their daily lives, which is so important when potty training. Teaching the difference between right and wrong, encouraging good table manners, and promoting positive food habits are also vital steps in the run-up to potty training as they help to promote your toddler's independence, making them feel grown up and keen to please.

### A little word for the grown-ups

My biggest tip for the terrible twos is to get your toddler involved in lots of simple tasks you need to do. Encourage them to throw their own nappy/pull-up in the bin in the morning – this helps to make them feel special and grown-up, and toddlers always love to be little helpers. Giving them some independence is a great way to avoid tantrums!

# Regression

Having the odd accident during the first month of potty training should not be classed as regression – true regression is when your little one continues to have multiple accidents daily and shows no interest in using the potty/toilet whatsoever. If your toddler does start to have accidents, you should be understanding, sympathetic and patient. It will upset them having accidents as much as it upsets you, so try to stay calm and do not make a huge issue out of it – this will only make the situation a lot worse. Try to say something positive, such as: 'Oh dear, never mind – that was a silly accident.' Potty training is new to your little one and is a lot to take in, and if they are tired or distracted accidents may happen. Go back to using the magic reward box and magic stars again with a fresh new approach for the incentives – such as changing the magical prizes – to further encourage your little one and bring the fun back into potty training.

I know it can be very tempting to put nappies/pull-ups back on your child when they start having regular accidents, but this can lead to very mixed messages and will only confuse your little trainer, so I really do advise you to stick to big boy/girl pants so your child does not regress any further.

Go back to the beginning of my programme and keep prompting your little trainer to ask if they need to use the potty/toilet, and they will pick it back up again. Remember that what you did before worked, so just reinforce the routine again. It will do no harm to sit your toddler down and explain again that they are a big boy/girl and we do not do wees or poos in our pants anymore.

Continue to use encouraging, positive language and hold your temper.

If your little one attends a childcare setting and you have seen regression, it is a good idea to make an appointment to discuss this with their key worker. It could be a result of something that has changed that is out of your control, such as your little one having friendship problems at nursery or feeling unwell.

Regression is very common in potty training so try not to worry if your toddler suddenly starts having accidents or refuses to use the potty/toilet. Just the slightest change in a toddler's life – no matter how small it may appear to us – can be a big thing in their little world, making them very anxious, which can lead to regression. This could be something that has happened at nursery, a new family member or a change at home, or simply them feeling under the weather. It is always good to try to find the source of your toddler's regression if you can, though I appreciate that trying to figure out a little person is not always easy!

## A new baby

Having a new baby in the family can have a huge impact on a toddler's potty training. In the eyes of a toddler the baby is getting all the attention, so for them to gain attention they start having accidents or may insist on wearing a nappy like the baby. This can be a very testing time for parents, especially as you may also be very sleep-deprived with a newborn in the house. In my experience this is a good time to reintroduce a reward system to help your toddler feel super special again, explaining to them that they can get rewards because they are a big boy/girl and the rewards are only for them, not the baby.

It's important to get your little one back on track as soon as possible. Even letting toddlers help change the baby's nappy is something I have found can help, and using phrases such as 'You're such a big boy/girl for helping Mummy/Daddy with your baby brother/sister' works too.

**Q**: I had a baby six weeks ago and my three-year-old daughter was doing so well with potty training. However, all of a sudden she is asking for a nappy again. Why is this, and what can I do, as I'm at my wits' end? She did so well for so long.

**A**: This is something I come across on a very regular basis. Your daughter's regression is a clear sign that a new baby has arrived and, through no fault of her own, is getting a lot of Mummy/Daddy's attention.

One of the things I've noticed over the years is that toddlers seem to really pick up on their parents changing the baby's nappy. This is something that normally takes some time to do and little ones are very clever at realising this and deciding that they want their nappy back on just like the baby – and therefore getting more of Mummy/Daddy's attention. I would suggest that you try to change your baby's nappy away from your toddler if possible and, when you have some one-to-one time with your daughter, say to her: 'What a big girl you are as you don't need nappies anymore. They are for babies. And you are Mummy's special big girl.' Try saying to her 'You can't have your nappy because you are too big now and we don't have any that will fit you.'

This is a very emotional and testing time for the whole family, and you can very easily lose your patience with your toddler. Try not to get cross as this will only aggravate the situation. Having a little extra support from family and friends can be very helpful during this period, so don't be afraid to ask for help. Phone calls of encouragement from grandparents to your little one can really help too. Try to give your daughter little jobs that help you with the baby to make her feel extra special, and offer a little reward, such as a magic star in order to gain a special little treat of her choice, for her efforts.

## Starting potty training too soon

Lots of parents choose to start potty training because of peer pressure from family, friends or childcare settings, and therefore start the potty training process when they feel they *should* do it, rather than when their toddler is showing all the correct signs of readiness. In my experience, starting potty training too early will only lead to frustration and regression. I cannot emphasise enough how important it is to listen to and watch your toddler for the key signs of readiness (see page 29) if you want to achieve successful training.

If you find that your child is having a huge amount of accidents I would advise booking an appointment with your doctor to rule out any health issues, such as a urinary tract infection or constipation (see pages 133 and 140). If your child does not have an underlying health concern and the regression lasts for a few weeks, I would advise only at this stage to revert back to nappies/pull-ups for a couple of weeks and then start the whole process again. Sometimes if potty training doesn't work it can be because your little one just isn't ready and you have started training a bit too early.

# Delayed Learning

I have been approached on many occasions for help with children with learning delays. Autism, Asperger's or other conditions such as ADHD affect a child's communication, behaviour and interaction, which can make potty training a very difficult task. I have tried many different ways and techniques over the years to see what works best and, though every condition is different, I have found that children with or without learning delays need and react well to a consistent approach. Children with learning delays may not show many signs of readiness and some will show none, so it will be down to you as the parent to make a judgement when you feel your little one is ready.

Most autistic children don't have the motivation to want to use the potty/toilet or even be like their friends or Mummy/Daddy, so potty training needs to be about you taking your time to find out what does and doesn't work for your child. Observe times when your child goes for a wee or poo and try to form a plan from this, developing a routine of set times throughout the day to prompt your child to use the potty/toilet.

My potty training programme has worked for many children with learning delays so do not assume your child cannot be trained. However, it's worth bearing in mind that it generally takes a little longer for them to get to grips with it. I have found throughout many years of training children with learning delays that they have a clearer understanding if everything is the same, using coloured rewards that are coordinated with their pants, for example. In my experience this has proven to be very successful. It's also important to make sure your child's pants are made from soft cotton and always cut the labels out as this is a notorious distraction for many children on the autism spectrum. Generally, you need to take a more persistent and thoughtful uniformed approach if your child has learning delays.

**Q**: My little girl is not interested in going on the potty and is showing no signs of readiness. She is over three years old and is on the autism spectrum. She also attends nursery. Once in a while she has sat on the toilet when I asked her to, and I praised her when she did, but she just doesn't seem very interested in getting her nappy off yet.

**A**: I would make an appointment with your daughter's nursery school and speak to her key worker to find out if she is showing any interest while she is with them. I would advise that you and the nursery will have to work together to devise a programme that you can both consistently implement. Try offering her some flashcards (see page 45) which may help get the message across and aid her understanding. It may be that she is just not grasping the concept yet or is a little bit delayed in her understanding.

Do make sure you wait for your child to show signs of readiness before implementing the programme as it will make the whole potty training process a lot less stressful for you both. I recommend that you purchase a potty, trainer seat and step stool in your child's favourite colour. I once worked with a boy who only liked green things, so I used green pants, green stars and a green potty and trainer seat. By pulling down his green pants and doing a wee or poo in his green potty, the boy was rewarded with a matching green star. The boy followed my programme through colour and responded in a calm and understanding way. I believe that because everything was the same colour, the programme was easier for him to follow. The matching colours helped to make it clear what he had to do and he didn't feel bombarded or overwhelmed by lots of different coloured products and stickers.

I suggest that you follow my five-day programme outlined in Chapter 4 though be aware that things may take a little longer for a child with learning delays. I would recommend using stars and the magic reward box rather than stickers and a reward chart as the box will be easier for your child to understand. Again, use stars in one colour only and, once you have chosen your child's favourite colour, create the stars together putting their name on them. Show your little one the stars dropping into the box so they understand where they go. It is important to reward your child with a star if they are willing to sit on the potty/toilet and follow my general guide on rewards outlined on page 42.

When it comes to praise I have found that some little ones do not like clapping or cheering – those with sensory processing disorder are particularly very sensitive – so be sure to choose the praise your child most enjoys. A big smile and a thumbs up is always a winner and, of course, a magic star in their favourite colour. I have found that children with learning delays always respond well to lots of cuddles and using basic language like 'It's potty time' or 'It's toilet time' with a warm smile always works well too.

I like to make the bathroom a warm, fun and interesting place for children. Make a sign with your child's name on it in their favourite colour (that matches their pants, potty, etc.) and hang it on the door. Also choose a fun hand soap for your child, making sure it's not heavily scented. Try using a soft light bulb so the bathroom is inviting and make sure the room is not cold. Avoid using strong-smelling cleaning products as many children – with or without learning delays – can find the smell overwhelming and it can put them off using the toilet. It's really useful to have a basket of toys or distractions in the bathroom that you know your little one will gravitate towards, such as bubbles to blow, textured objects or stretchy toys. This will help to relax your child and keep them sitting on the potty/toilet for longer. Keep these toys just for use in the bathroom so your child associates them with using the potty/toilet.

Try not to let your little one rush off the potty/toilet too soon – one tip is to count the fingers on their hands to delay them, just to make sure there is nothing more to come out. You may want to flush the toilet yourself after they have left as some little ones are scared of the flushing noise.

Flashcards are fantastic for children with learning delays as they generally relate to pictures better than to commands. You can either buy flashcards or make your own (see page 45). Stick some of them on the wall above the areas that relate to the image (you might want to laminate them you need to ensure they are splash proof!) For example, the 'good girl/boy washing their hands' card could go above the sink, and the 'good girl/boy sitting on the toilet' card could be placed above the toilet. Keep some cards loose so that you can use them to prompt your child to do some of the tasks, such as showing them the wee or poo in the toilet, followed by flushing the toilet, and putting their big boy/girl pants on. Flashcards are a great way of communicating to your child throughout the day and, if they have an accident, you can use them to show your little one where the wee or poo should go. Finish by showing them the magic reward box and well done flashcards, and follow up with the actual box and stars. This will help to reinforce the message and excitement of getting a reward.

Though every child is different, I have found that all the little trainers I have worked with have really taken to and understand the coloured magic stars, potty training flashcards and the colour-coordinated big boy/girl pants. I believe this works because the child associates everything in that particular chosen colour with going on the potty/toilet. Using my programme consistently every day and keeping to a strict routine definitely works for these little trainers. Just be aware that it can take a little time for them to get the hang of it.

## A little word for the grown-ups

Try not to be overwhelmed by all this information. It is here to give you the confidence and reassurance you need to feel one step ahead of those wees and poos because, believe me, our children sometimes like to test us!

# 7 Your Little One's Health

oddlers are very prone to catching bugs, especially
when in a childcare setting. This can affect potty
training as, when little ones feel unwell, it can upset
their concentration and routine. If your toddler is really
quite poorly with a tummy bug, flu or virus then you
may have to revert back to nappies/pull-ups for this short
period, but you must explain to your little one that it is just
because they are very poorly.

## Urinary Tract Infections

f your child suddenly starts to have consistent accidents
it may well be a sign of a urinary tract infection (UTI).

Keep an eye on the colour and smell of their wee. If it is cloudy in colour and foul-smelling, this can indicate a UTI. Other signs that your toddler may have a UTI include:

- Complaining that it hurts or burns when they wee.
- Wincing or becoming upset while they are weeing.
- A high temperature.
- Lack of energy.
- Pain in their tummy.

Consult your doctor if your child has any of these symptoms.

There are so many ways a toddler can get a UTI. Cystitis is a common type of UTI and one that many grils get. Cystitis is far more common in girls than in boys, and one of the reasons for this is because they wipe from back to front and the dirty toilet paper carries bacteria from the bottom to the urethra. It is very important to teach girls to wipe the correct way: *from front to back*, even after a wee. Try to avoid using heavily scented soap or perfumed bubble bath as these can all play a part in increasing the likelihood of cystitis and other UTIs.

If you suspect your toddler has a UTI then you should make an appointment to see your doctor as soon as possible. Urinary tract infections are not usually serious and can be treated effectively with antibiotics.

# Diarrhoea

Diarrhoea is something we have probably all experienced and everyone will agree that it's not very pleasant at all. By the time your little one reaches the age of five they are sure to have experienced this. Diarrhoea can be very distressing and embarrassing for a toddler because of the lack of warning, drama and mess it brings with it.

If your child has more than five loose, watery poos in a day then it is usually a sign that they have diarrhoea. It is important to show no stress if your toddler has diarrhoea and to clean and change them as quickly as possible. Most importantly, always reassure your toddler that it is not their fault.

If you are in the middle of potty training and your little one is becoming very stressed because they have diarrhoea I would, on this occasion, suggest putting a nappy/pull-up back on and explaining to them that this is just a temporary measure until the diarrhoea has stopped. If your toddler is not stressed by the diarrhoea and is still willing to sit on the potty/toilet then stick to the pants and keep going with the potty training. It will be down to you to judge how your little one is feeling. Some toddlers can become very tired and quite unwell with diarrhoea – they can sleep more or be grumpier – while others are not bothered by it at all. As I always say, each child is different, so follow your little one's cues.

## Causes

Diarrhoea can be caused by many different things, even constipation. I know this may sound contradictory as we all associate constipation with solid, hard poos but, in fact, diarrhoea can be the overflow of poo leaking out in liquid form around the blockage, with no warning at all. Diarrhoea can also indicate the start of a tummy bug, or is a sign that your toddler has eaten food that has caused a bacterial infection. If you notice that diarrhoea occurs after your little one eats a certain food, speak with your doctor as it could be a sign of a food intolerance or allergy and they can investigate the cause.

## Symptoms

- Doing over five poos a day which are watery and can be smelly.
- Complaining of a tummy ache and sickness.

- More smelly wind than usual.
- Wet brown stains in your toddler's pants or nappy/pull-up.

## Treatment

- Make sure your little one drinks plenty of fluid – water is always best, though watered-down sugar-free squash is also fine. Keep offering your toddler little sips of fluid as it's so important to keep them hydrated. Diarrhoea can lead to dehydration, which can be very dangerous. Keep an eye on the colour of your toddler's wee – if it's light and clear then they are hydrated, but if it's dark and very yellow then they need more liquid.
- Offer your little one plain food such as boiled chicken or fish, and starchy foods such as mashed potato, pasta, white bread, white rice and plain crackers. Bananas are also good.
- Avoid sugary drinks, especially drinks that contain sweeteners, fruit juice, (particularly apple juice) and fizzy drinks as these can make diarrhoea much worse.
- Avoid any food that contains artificial sweeteners, such as chocolate, sugary cereals and sweets, and do not give your toddler dairy products, fatty fried foods or processed foods, as these can all exacerbate diarrhoea.
- Ensure your little one gets plenty of rest.

## Signs of dehydration

- Dry, cracked lips.
- Dry mouth.
- Less frequent wees that are dark in colour.
- Becoming drowsy and irritable.
- Cold and blotchy-looking hands and feet.
- Low energy levels, seeming very weak or limp.
- No tears when crying.

Give your little one fluid in small sips as often as you can, increasing the fluid as they become more hydrated again. Your pharmacist may also recommend oral rehydration sachets. If the above symptoms continue or you are at all concerned, please seek immediate medical advice.

## Prevention

Diarrhoea is highly contagious so it is really important that you try to do all you can to prevent it and avoid it spreading. You cannot be fussy enough when it comes to diarrhoea in your house.

Make sure everyone in the family washes their hands thoroughly with warm water and soap after using the toilet or stroking a pet, and before going anywhere near the kitchen, particularly before touching or preparing any food. A quick splash under the cold tap will not help prevent or stop the spread of diarrhoea! In particular make sure that your little one washes their hands and even give them their own little hand towel. Disinfect all toilet seats daily wearing protective gloves and also wipe over door handles.

If you are resorting back to nappies/pull-ups during this spell of diarrhoea, make sure you bag these up and put them straight in the outside bin to help stop the spread of germs.

Do not send your little one to their childcare setting for at least 48 hours after their last spell of diarrhoea. Once they do go back, make sure you inform the setting that they have been unwell.

## Tips to avoid diarrhoea

- If you're travelling abroad with your little one always use bottled water to avoid upset tummies.
- Always get your little one to wash their hands. Lack of basic hygiene is arguably one of the biggest causes of diarrhoea.
- Always wash fruit and vegetables thoroughly before eating.

# Constipation

Constipation is very common in toddlers, especially once they start potty training. This can make potty training stressful, but rest-assured that it's usually short-lived.

## Causes

### Dehydration

Toddlers need to keep well-hydrated, as if they do not drink enough fluid their poos will become harder – the body absorbs all the fluid from whatever they eat or drink, leaving nothing to keep the poo moist. Toddlers can go through phases when they don't drink enough, so you need to keep an eye on this and make sure you keep encouraging your little one to drink throughout the day. If they are at a child-care setting make sure you ask the staff to keep giving your toddler water, especially if you think your toddler won't ask for it when they are far too busy playing and having fun.

## *Anxiety around potty training*

I come across this every day with my little trainers and it is a very common cause of constipation. Little ones often refuse to do a poo on the potty/toilet at the beginning of potty training. This is something that has to be worked on using extra encouragement to give them the confidence to go (see page 108 for more advice on this). Toddlers can become anxious and feel pressured if parents constantly ask them if they need a poo. This can result in them deliberately holding their poo in (also known as 'withholding'). To change this I encourage toddlers to sit on the potty/toilet after mealtimes and keep them entertained to try to make light of it. Try to keep them relaxed for at least 10 minutes if you can. If this doesn't work, just reassure your little one and ask them to tell you when they need a poo. Keep a nappy/pull-up in the bathroom and say to them 'You can do it in there.' Once you have taken their nappy/pull-up off and flushed the poo down the toilet together, ensure they wash their hands and put their pants back on. Keep going with this until their confidence is back – bear in mind that this can take up to two weeks depending on how your little one is responding. Every child is different so it may take more or less time.

## *Diet*

It's not uncommon for toddlers to be fussy at this stage about what they eat, so getting the correct foods into them can be tricky. It can also be hard to break the habit of them drinking huge amounts of milk, which can fill them up resulting in them not getting enough high-fibre foods, such as vegetables, fruit and wholegrains. Try to reduce your toddler's milk intake gradually and up their intake of high-fibre foods (see page 160). If your little one is a cheese monster and suffering with constipation, limit the amount they eat as cheese can exacerbate the problem.

### Foods to avoid for constipation

- Processed foods, such as ready meals (fresh or frozen).
- Fried chips.
- White pasta and rice.
- Excess sweets.
- An overload of dairy products.
- Too much white bread.

## *Poor toileting position*

A poor toileting position can really hamper your toddler when they are doing a poo. It's important to encourage your little one to sit properly on the potty/toilet to encourage those poos to come out (see page 39).

## *A change in circumstances*

A change in your little one's routine, such as a recent holiday or change of childcare setting, can also cause constipation. Toddlers can be so sensitive at this age, becoming anxious and upset easily, which can have an effect on their tummies.

## Symptoms

- Loss of appetite.
- Pooing only two or three times a week.
- Their poo is in separate small hard lumps, or a large lumpy poo in a sausage shape that is hard to pass (see page 144).
- Complaining of a sore tummy.
- Bloated, distended tummy.
- Wet brown stains in their pants or nappy/pull-up. This can be a sign that they have a solid poo stuck and liquid poo is leaking out around the sides of it.
- Getting upset when they have a poo.

---

### A WEE fact for grown-ups

It is important not just for toddlers, but for us grown-ups to try to maintain a healthy bowel and bladder. Try checking how healthy your poos are!

---

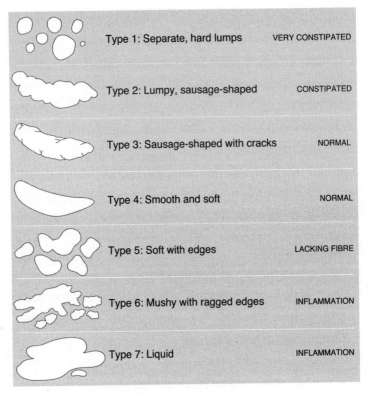

Type 1: Separate, hard lumps — VERY CONSTIPATED

Type 2: Lumpy, sausage-shaped — CONSTIPATED

Type 3: Sausage-shaped with cracks — NORMAL

Type 4: Smooth and soft — NORMAL

Type 5: Soft with edges — LACKING FIBRE

Type 6: Mushy with ragged edges — INFLAMMATION

Type 7: Liquid — INFLAMMATION

What our poos tell us

## Prevention

### Exercise

Regular exercise is so important – keeping your little one active is key to maintaining a healthy bowel and it's the same for us adults too. A little walk to the park or a swim will help to keep the bowel moving and encourage food through the digestive system.

## Regular toilet trips

Gently remind your toddler to use the potty/toilet regularly, especially after a meal. Try to get them to sit for at least 10 minutes at a time on the potty/toilet. Relax them by grabbing a book or bubbles as this will help to keep them sitting for longer. Have a daily toilet routine and stick to it.

## Position

Squatting is the best way to get those poos out (see page 39). If your little one is using a potty, try to encourage them to lean forward with their hands on their thighs, making sure their knees are bent and firmly on the ground. If your little one is using a trainer seat or the toilet then a step stool is perfect to help with correct positioning.

## Eat together

Try to have at least one meal a day together as a family. This will help encourage your toddler to eat the foods they need for a healthy bowel and have a wider variety. Small regular meals with the correct nutrition are important. Remember, it's about quality not quantity.

**Q**: Is it okay to give my son laxatives to help soften his poo as I think he is constipated?

**A**: Firstly, I would never suggest giving little ones any form of medication without the advice of a doctor. If you think your son has constipation there are many things you can do at home to try to alleviate this. Make sure he is getting enough fluid and introduce a high-fibre diet with plenty of vegetables, fruit and wholegrain foods. Get your son to do a little more exercise to help get his bowels moving. Nice warm baths and a rub of the tummy can also help. If your son does try to go for a poo on the potty, make sure his legs are slightly raised with his feet on the ground as this will help him release any stored poos. Use a step stool for poos on the toilet to ensure correct positioning. If this still doesn't work then I would take him to the doctor, who may prescribe some medication.

Constipation in toddlers is very rarely serious. However, if you have tried all of the above or if your toddler has a high temperature or is vomiting or losing weight then you should consult your doctor. If the constipation persists then your doctor may prescribe some temporary medication, such as mild laxatives, if they feel it is necessary.

> ## A little word for the grown-ups
>
> Constipation or diarrhoea are quite common in toddlers (as well as adults) and can come on very quickly, but they can be easily treated at home. If your child is under the weather it may affect potty training slightly, but it's important to keep going with your usual routine as much as possible.

# Threadworms

Threadworms can spread really quickly and are very common in younger children. Threadworms spread when their eggs are ingested and can pass to other people through hands, surfaces, bed linen, towels, toilet seats, lunch tables and sand pits. They are very easily passed on when people touch these surfaces and then touch their mouths. Do not worry if your little one has worms as they do not cause any major harm, but they do need to be treated as soon as possible which can be done at home. Having worms could really upset potty training too, because your little one might experience abdominal cramps, nausea and loss of appetite. If your child attends a childcare setting, make sure you inform the setting so they can take any necessary steps.

## Symptoms

The most obvious sign that your little one has worms is an itchy bottom and very restless sleep at night. Worms tend to move around more at night to lay their eggs, which obviously disturbs the little one's sleep. In girls watch out as they can spread to the vagina and can cause a discharge. You can often spot worms in your child's nappy/pull-up or in the potty/toilet once your child has done a poo – they are like a very thin white thread. Threadworms can even be found on the potty or toilet seat after a toddler has sat on it.

## Treatment

As soon as you spot your little one has worms you need to go to your local pharmacy and ask for an over-the-counter treatment. Treatment comes in the form of chewable tablets, or you can ask for a liquid if you think that will be easier for your little one to take. It is important to treat the whole family to avoid the worms spreading further. It is normal for the itching to continue for a few days, so you may need to use a cream, such as Sudocrem, to soothe your little one's bottom. Make sure you wash all towels and bed linen and disinfect toilets and all surfaces in the home. Don't shake towels or bedding as this can cause the eggs to spread. If your child has had worms once, there is a likelihood they may get them again, so it's important to keep an eye out.

## Prevention

Threadworms is one of the reasons why it is so important to teach little ones the importance of hand washing from a young age – and not just after using the bathroom, but also after attending nursery, playing outside and before eating any food. Make sure your toddler has clean underwear every day and a daily bath or shower. A clean set of pyjamas every couple of days is also key, as is a weekly change of bed linen. Try to keep your toddler's fingernails short as they can harbour many germs.

# Nappy Rash

Nappy rash is something many little ones get in their younger life. Though it is not common in newborns, nappy rash can become a problem after a few months of age, right the way up to toddlerhood. If your little one does have nappy rash you will be able to see it immediately and it is generally easy to treat. Nappy rash can look like red patches on your little one's bottom and it feels hot to the touch. It can also come in the form of blisters.

Not all nappy rash will affect little ones, but some can get very sore and it will make them unsettled and upset. It can also distress them when they go for a wee or poo, and they can become very upset when their nappy/pull-up is changed as it can be painful for them.

If your little one does have nappy rash and you are thinking of starting potty training you must get this cleared up first as it will only delay the process otherwise.

## Typical causes of nappy rash

- Prolonged contact with wee or poo on your little one's skin.
- Not keeping your little one's bottom clean and dry.
- Using cheap, less absorbent nappies/pull-ups that leave the skin damp.
- Using wet wipes that have a strong alcohol content or are heavily perfumed.
- Using perfumed soap or bubble bath.

- Sensitivity to a product you have used on your little one's bottom.
- Antibiotics can sometimes cause nappy rash and thrush.
- Diarrhoea can also cause nappy rash as the enzymes in diarrhoea are more active than in healthy poo.

## Treatment

Nappy rash can be easily treated at home if it's mild and your little one is not too distressed by it. However, if they are quite upset then you should ask your pharmacist or health visitor for advice.

Nappy rash will usually clear up after a few days, but if it persists and you are concerned always consult your doctor for advice. If your little one is in a childcare setting please advise them about the nappy rash so they can follow your treatment routine.

### Barrier cream

Apply a thin layer of barrier cream to your little one's clean bottom after a nappy change or bath. This will protect their skin and shield it from wee and poo sitting against it. Barrier creams are widely available so just ask your pharmacist for advice on which one to buy.

### Change nappies/pull-ups regularly

Do not leave your little one in a soiled nappy/pull-up. Wet or dirty nappies/pull-ups need to be changed regularly. Try not to buy cheap nappies/pull-ups that will leave your little one wet and uncomfortable. Check out the reviews before purchasing or speak to other parents for recommendations.

### Clean your child's bottom

I always recommend using cotton wool with lukewarm water or alcohol-free wipes to clean a child's bottom. Make sure you clean the whole area and always wipe from front to back. It is also important to pat the area dry.

### Have nappy-free time

Little ones love nappy-free time and it's so good to let some air get to their skin. If your child is little then lay them on a towel or changing mat on the floor and let them kick around for a while without their nappy/pull-up on. If your child is a toddler, let them run around for a while with no nappy/pull-up on or just wearing a pair of cotton pants. It's really good to let their skin breathe. Remember to remind your toddler that they have no nappy/pull-up on. They may have a little accident or two, but this can be expected as they are used to their nappy/pull-up acting as a safeguard.

### Bath your child daily

We all love that wonderful smell of a clean baby/toddler but try to avoid perfumed soap and bubble bath or perfumed cream and talcum powder as these can further irritate little ones' delicate skin. I always recommend bathing your child daily but if they have nappy rash and it is very sore, just give them a gentle wash until it clears.

## A little note for the grown-ups

Most little ones will get nappy rash at some point in their lives so don't think it's your fault and blame yourself. Young children have such sensitive skin and even the simplest thing can trigger it. I was fortunate that my children only suffered from mild nappy rash and I put this down to the fact that I only ever used cotton wool pads and lukewarm water to wash their little bums!

# 8 Your Little One's Diet

From the age of two toddlers can start to become very fussy about what they eat, and foods they used to love and eat suddenly get rejected. This is something the majority of toddlers will go through, but it's important to try to turn it around. If your little one is not getting the nutrients they need in their daily diet it can drastically affect their digestive system, which can lead to constipation and, in turn, put pressure on the bladder leading to wee accidents. It's important that we get our toddlers used to a good variety of meals and to love their food, because a bad diet can lead to toileting accidents, which we definitely want to avoid if we can.

It's important to realise how food can affect the daily lives of toddlers and it is our job as parents to make sure we help guide them so that they enjoy their food. Toddlers can pick up so much from their parents, so if there is something you don't like to eat, it's important that you don't discuss this in front of your little one, otherwise they will have an instant dislike to it even if they haven't tried it!

Food fussiness can be so frustrating for parents as often it's hard to understand what has changed. We all hear stories about how toddlers will only eat pasta with cheese or chips, and we can all be very judgemental about this until we find ourselves with our own toddler doing exactly the same thing! My experience of helping toddlers overcome this fussy stage has shown me that, again, it's all about seeing things through their eyes. We as adults wouldn't like to have food shoved in our faces and be made to eat it, and the same applies for toddlers. It's all about letting them have a certain amount of control – a bit like potty training. What I have learnt is that you need to find out what your little one does like to eat rather than forcing them to eat what they don't.

The best advice I can give you to try to overcome food fussiness is to start by making snacks or lunches with your little one, getting them involved and teaching them about different foods. This really does work. It will make your toddler feel very special and this in turn encourages them to try different foods. Try not to offer huge amounts of choice in the first instance; maybe have a few colourful ingredients, obviously including veggies or fruit. Be creative with your toddler and make faces out of bread, using carrot sticks for hair and cucumber for ears – toddlers absolutely love this. Get your child to taste the food while you are making it using lots of encouraging words, such as 'Mmmm that's yummy isn't it?' or 'That will make you grow into a big girl/boy!'

Letting toddlers handle their own food and feed themselves is also key to overcoming fussiness, though obviously they need to be supervised. Your little one is becoming very independent at this age and should now be feeding themselves, so make sure you are not spoon-feeding them anymore as they are more likely to reject the food if it seems that you're forcing them. Make sure your child is sitting at a table at mealtimes as food should only be served when they are sitting down. This so important – not only for a routine and teaching them table manners, but also to avoid choking. Toddlers still only have very small tummies so don't expect them to eat huge portions or clear their plate. Serving three small meals a day with healthy snacks in between works much better than expecting your toddler to eat mammoth portions in one sitting. If your toddler is still drinking large quantities of milk this can also have an effect on their food intake as lots of milk can make them feel full, so try to gradually reduce their milk intake if you can.

I have always loved mealtimes in my home and at least once a day we eat as a family. This is such a special time and it's so important for little ones to watch their family enjoying food together. For those of you who work full-time and struggle to get home for mealtimes, try to find time at the weekend to make this happen. And remember that those little ones who are at nursery will be benefitting from sitting with their friends while eating. Make sure that if you eat dinner together, it isn't too late for your toddler as if they become tired they will be less interested in eating. You'll also need to exercise a little patience while they are eating as some little ones do take forever! It's important not to rush them so that they have time to chew their food properly and enjoy their time doing so. They need to think of mealtimes as happy occasions rather than stressful ones.

If your child rejects a certain food, or suddenly takes a dislike to it, keep slowly trying to reintroduce it into their diet without a fuss. It can often take up to 15 times for a new food to be accepted by a toddler, so do persist. If your toddler still dislikes it after numerous attempts that's fine – we can't all like everything. If your child pushes the food away then just take the plate away and try not to react – simply say, 'Okay, thank you.'

Although it's obviously better for toddlers to love their food at face value, sometimes we need to disguise certain foods just so we can give them the vitamins and nutrients they need. This is easy to do by blending vegetables and adding them to dishes such as pasta sauce, mashed potato, shepherd's pie or soup, so they don't even realise they are eating them. This is a great way of introducing the taste of certain vegetables to your child and, in time, you can introduce them to the whole vegetable.

## Sugar

We all know that little ones can be partial to sweet things, but a diet with a high sugar content can lead to diarrhoea or constipation, which is not comfortable, especially if your child is beginning to potty train. Foods with a high sugar content also contribute to tooth decay, obesity and diabetes, and they can really affect your little one's mood. As I'm sure many of you have experienced, sugar can trigger hyperactive behaviour, this can make it very tricky for little ones to listen and follow simple instructions, which is a big issue when you are trying to introduce potty training. Little ones can easily get into the habit of eating sweet sugary foods which can also contribute to making them fussy eaters when it comes to savoury foods. A chocolate bar can be more appealing to a toddler than a piece of broccoli! A little treat now and again is fine, but try to encourage your little one's taste buds with savoury food rather than sugar. Restrict sugary treats and offer your toddler some yummy flavoured rice cakes, breadsticks or organic cheesy snacks instead.

# Fibre

Try to keep your little one's diet as varied as possible and ensure you include fibre in each of their meals to keep their bowels working nicely. If you find that your little one has a high-fibre diet but is constipated, it could be a sign that they are having too much fibre. Try to keep a diary of what they are eating during the day and adjust the fibre content accordingly. If you are still experiencing problems, I suggest going to see your health visitor or doctor.

Constipation in toddlers is very common, and most of the time it can be due to something they are lacking in their diet or because they are not drinking enough fluid. The bladder and the bowel are so closely linked that they can easily upset each other if they are not treated properly. Below are some of the foods that little bodies need that will help to promote a healthy bowel:

- Plenty of water.
- Fish (poached or baked, not fried).
- Lean, grilled meats.
- Wholegrain bread, wholewheat pasta and brown rice – these have lots of fibre that promotes a healthy bowel.
- Broccoli, spinach and other greens – around 100g of cooked broccoli can provide a good portion of your toddler's fibre and vitamin C.

- Baked sweet or white potato (skin-on for extra fibre).
- Beans (e.g. baked or kidney).
- Avocado.
- Edamame beans – toddlers love these as they can pop the little peas out of the pods!.
- Air-popped popcorn – this is high in fibre and makes a great snack for toddlers. It is not too high in calories and most little ones love it.
- Pears.
- Plums.
- Apples.
- Berries, such as blueberries, strawberries, raspberries and blackberries.
- Kiwi fruit.
- Prunes.
- Peaches.

# Toddler-Friendly Recipes

I have included below some simple recipes that are high in fibre and essential vitamins and minerals to keep your little one's bowel healthy. I used to make these with my own children – yes, it made a lot of mess and took twice as long, but these were precious times and now my children appreciate their food and have a love of cooking. Remember to wash all fruit and vegetables before cooking.

## Smoothies

Smoothies are a perfect way to get healthy fruit and vegetables into your little one without them knowing! You can add almost anything to a smoothie and the ingredients do not have to be expensive. Shop around as some supermarkets do some amazing prices on fruit, and you can also buy frozen fruit and veg as they have the same amount of nutrients as fresh produce. Cute little cups with lids and straws are widely available and don't cost a lot – I've found that these really encourage little ones to drink so they are well worth the money.

Smoothies are easy to make and are a great way of combating constipation. Try adding some chia seeds, hemp seeds or avocado to the smoothies – this will all help to keep your little one's bowels moving nicely. Smoothies are great for breakfast to kick-start the day or as a snack, but beware they can be quite filling for little tummies.

Here are a few smoothie recipes I have used with toddlers to get their bowels moving:

★

## Apple Berry Smoothie

### Serves 3–4

2 bananas, peeled
1 large apple, cored and sliced (skin on)
300g frozen raspberries
75ml water

Place all the ingredients in a blender and whizz. Blend the mixture until it is smooth and creamy. If it is too thick, add some more water. The mixture can be kept in the fridge covered for up to a day, but give it a good stir before drinking.

★

## Very Blueberry Smoothie

### Serves 3–4

150g blueberries
150ml natural yoghurt
1 tsp runny honey
75ml water
75g ice cubes
1 banana, peeled (optional – for a thicker consistency)

Place all the ingredients in a blender and whizz. Blend the mixture until it is smooth and creamy. If it is too thick, add some more water or ice. If it is too thin, add the banana. The mixture can be kept in the fridge covered for up to a day, but give it a good stir before drinking.

★

## Peachy Bottom Smoothie

### Serves 3–4

1 large peach, peeled, halved and pitted
150g blueberries
75g seedless grapes (green or red)
75ml water
150g ice cubes

Place all the ingredients in a blender and whizz. Blend the mixture until it is smooth and creamy. If it is too thick, add some more water or ice. The mixture can be kept in the fridge covered for up to a day, but give it a good stir before drinking.

★

## Strawberry Burst Smoothie

### Serves 3–4

150g strawberries, hulled (fresh or frozen)
75g fresh spinach

2 tbsp runny honey
150ml water
75g ice cubes

Place all the ingredients in a blender and whizz. Blend the mixture until it is smooth and creamy. If it is too thick, add some more water or ice. The mixture can be kept in the fridge covered for up to a day, but give it a good stir before drinking.

# Breakfast, Lunch and Dinner Treats

I have always enjoyed making my little ones' food look fun and inviting to encourage them to eat what is on their plate. Making meals interesting and fun, as well as healthy, is essential for successful potty training as what little ones put in their mouths will affect their toileting habits. Making meals with your toddler is also a good way for them to learn about food.

★

## Healthy and Easy Pancakes

These pancakes only require seven ingredients and they freeze well – perfect for busy parents! They are also fun to eat and nutritious for growing toddlers. They help to maintain a healthy diet, which is ideal when potty training.

### Makes 12 mini pancakes

1 medium egg
150ml whole milk
150g wholewheat flour
1 tsp baking powder
a handful of strawberries or blueberries, or 1 banana or
apple (cored), chopped (optional)
2 tbsp unsalted butter, melted, plus extra for greasing
1 tbsp runny honey (optional)

Beat the egg in a bowl and mix in the milk. Add the flour, baking powder and fruit of your choice (if using) and mix well. Finally, stir in the melted butter.

Lightly grease a frying pan and heat over a medium heat. Drop 1 tablespoon of the pancake mixture into the pan. You might be able to fit two or three in at the same time.

Cook the pancakes until the tops have bubbles on them and the mixture is no longer shiny – about 45 seconds to 1 minute.

Flip the pancakes over and cook for an additional 45 seconds to 1 minute, until the bottoms are a light golden brown. Remove from the heat and set on a plate to cool. Repeat with the rest of the mixture. Serve with runny honey, if using.

★

## Fishy Fingers

Including fish in your little one's diet is great for their digestive system and helps maintain a healthy bowel. These are easy to make at home and very tasty.

**Serves up to 2 adults and 2 children**

1 large egg
100g wholemeal breadcrumbs
a drizzle of olive oil
500g skinless and boneless chunky white cod/haddock
or salmon, cut into thick strips

Preheat the oven to 200°C/180°C fan/gas 6.

Beat the egg in a bowl and tip the breadcrumbs on to a plate. Drizzle the olive oil onto a baking sheet.

Dip the fish strips into the egg, then coat them with the breadcrumbs. Transfer to the baking sheet.

Bake for 15–20 minutes until golden, turning them halfway through. Be careful when lifting the fish fingers off the sheet as they are very delicate. Serve with baked potatoes or homemade chips and vegetables.

**Tip:** Why not double the ingredients and freeze a batch for another time? Place the uncooked fish fingers into a plastic container with baking paper in between and place in the freezer. You can cook them straight from frozen – they should take 25–30 minutes.

★

## Hedgehog Mash

This was always a dinner my children loved. It is a great way of adding vegetables to a fussy eater's meal. The sausages can be replaced with carrots for the hedgehog's spine.

### Serves 4

1 tsp butter or margarine, plus extra for mashing
12 thin sausages
4 sweet or white potatoes, peeled and chopped into
small chunks
3 medium heads of broccoli, broken into florets
300g frozen petit pois

Preheat the oven to 180°C/160°C fan/gas 4.

Melt the butter or margarine in an ovenproof dish and add the sausages. Place the dish in the oven and cook for 30 minutes, turning the sausages halfway through.

Meanwhile, place the potatoes into a saucepan of water and boil for 20 minutes until soft. While the potatoes are boiling, place the broccoli into another saucepan of water and boil for 15 minutes until just tender.

Boil the petit pois for 5–6 minutes, or according to the packet instructions.

Once cooked, drain the potatoes and put them back into the saucepan. Add the broccoli, a little butter and mash with a potato masher until smooth.

Divide the mashed potato and broccoli mixture between four plates and form the mash into an oval shape (it does not have to be perfect!).

Remove the sausages from the oven and cut them in half. Stick the sausages randomly into the mash to resemble a hedgehog.

Drain the petit pois. Place two peas on to each mash hedgehog for the eyes and one for the nose to create a face. Place the remaining petit pois around the hedgehogs, and serve.

★

## Green Pasta

Wholewheat pasta is highly nutritious and high in fibre. When it's combined with avocado, it makes for a healthy and delicious meal for little ones.

### Serves 4

300g wholewheat pasta (in your child's favourite shape)
2 large avocados
1 tsp olive oil
150g grated cheddar cheese
100g grated Parmesan

Cook the pasta according to the packet instructions.

While the pasta is cooking, cut both avocados in half, destone them and scoop out the flesh. Mash the flesh in a bowl, drizzle with the olive oil and mix to make a smooth consistency. Cover to avoid the avocado turning brown.

Once the pasta is cooked, drain it leaving a tiny trace of cooking water in the pan. Return the pasta to the pan, add the grated cheddar and stir. Add the avocado mixture and mix well.

Place into bowls and sprinkle with Parmesan before serving.

**Tip:** This meal can be adapted by adding chicken or using broccoli instead of avocado.

★

## Pulpetti

This is a recipe that brings back many memories for me. I was taught this recipe when I was only four years old cooking with my Nana in Malta. As children we used to get so excited when we knew she was cooking these and she had to make 40 at a time as we would eat them before they got on the plate! This is a very traditional Maltese dish often made with the remains of roasted or boiled meat, but it can also be made with tuna, salmon and minced meat, and any vegetables can be added. I made these for my children when they were young and it was one of their favourites. I would like to share this recipe with you so you can try it with your little ones too. It is a great dish for hiding vegetables and adding extra fibre to relieve constipation.

### Makes 20 balls

3 large potatoes, peeled and chopped into large chunks

1 tbsp milk

1 egg, beaten

2 sprigs of fresh parsley, finely chopped (optional)

3 cooked skinless, chicken breasts (or salmon fillets), finely chopped or minced

75g breadcrumbs

75g plain flour

1 tbsp olive oil

Place the potatoes into a saucepan of water and boil for 20 minutes until soft. Drain the potatoes, place them back in the pan and mash them with the milk. Add the egg and parsley and stir well. Add the chicken and breadcrumbs and work the mixture together thoroughly.

Once mixed, form tiny round balls from the mixture and then flatten them out into an oval shape the size of a small pancake.

Place the flour in a shallow dish and dip both sides of the patties into the flour.

Heat the olive oil in a frying pan and gently cook the pulpetti until they are evenly browned on both sides. These are delicious served with fresh vegetables.

**Tip:** Uncooked pulpetti freeze well. Store in freezer bags, defrost thoroughly, and cook as above once thawed.

# 9 Frequently Asked Questions

E very child is unique and will come with their own training-related issues. However, over many years working with families and their little ones, I have encountered some common queries and concerns. I have included these below and hope that my solutions will help you on your own potty training journey.

## Should we start with a potty or go straight on the toilet with a trainer seat?

I get asked this question on a daily basis. After speaking to hundreds of parents it is usually down to their own preference rather than their toddler's, but I always recommend buying a potty *and* a trainer seat as this then gives your little one a choice; after all, it is them who will be training.

I have found that most toddlers gravitate towards the potty when they first start training as it is smaller and closer to the ground. It is also quicker for little ones to access and is easier to take out with you when you leave the home.

Your toddler will naturally transition from the potty to a trainer seat anyway, so it's good to have a seat on hand for when your toddler is ready. As I've said before, the potty and trainer seat do not have to be expensive, but I do recommend that you buy both. I have discovered that buying a potty and trainer seat in the same colour/pattern keeps the continuity going and toddlers respond very well to this.

## My daughter does not want to use a potty or trainer seat and just wants to sit directly on the toilet. Is this a problem?

There is no problem whatsoever with your daughter wanting to sit directly on the toilet. I always recommend going with whatever your little one gravitates towards as long as you get the results. I would recommend a step stool just to make it easier for her to access the toilet, help to stabilise her a bit more and maintain the correct squat position.

This is great as you will not have to transition from a potty or a trainer seat, but do be aware that if you are out and about some public toilets can be very unhygienic so make sure you are prepared with hand sanitiser and a mini sterilising spray just in case. Try to make sure your daughter uses the toilet before she leaves the house.

## Should we use pants or pull-ups?

I have potty trained many children over the years and have trialled several different methods using pull-ups, pants and no pants at all. I have found that using no pants definitely does not work, except that it means the toddler can sit down on the potty/toilet quickly and does not have to worry about pulling their pants down first.

Pull-ups are something that many parents gravitate towards and I have used them in the past when training little ones. I think pull-ups are very useful for when toddlers have a daytime nap or for long car journeys in the early stages of potty training. However, I do not like pull-ups to be used during the day while potty training as this gives toddlers very mixed messages. I understand that pull-ups are a very easy option for parents as they absorb some of the liquid and reduce lots of pant changes but, though this is a slightly less stressful option when potty training, it is also expensive and not one for making progress. Pull-ups are thin and soft so they feel comfortable to a toddler and make them feel like they are still in a nappy. If you train your child with pull-ups it can make the whole process a lot slower as your little one has the security of the pull-up, cannot feel the wetness and therefore does not feel the urgency in moving on in their training. In my experience, using pull-ups when potty training only makes life more difficult.

As you will have seen from my programme, I recommend using pants as soon as you start potty training. Your toddler will find it easier to understand the difference between wearing big boy/girl pants and a nappy/pull-up and, if your child does have an accident while they are wearing pants, they will quickly realise the difference as they can feel the wetness.

Potty training is a new stage in your toddler's development and I am a great believer in starting as you mean to go on – every child I have trained has definitely progressed a lot quicker wearing pants.

## My two-year-old has started taking his nappy off when he has done a wee and poo but his speech is very limited. Is it time to start potty training?

It is great that your son has started to realise when he has wet or soiled his nappy, but this is not enough to start potty training. At this stage, I would start using the words 'wee' and 'poo' in preparation for when he is fully ready. There are so many more signs of readiness he needs to be showing before you even consider starting potty training (see page 29). If you start too early and your son has no real understanding and cannot communicate clearly, this will only lead to a stressful time for you both.

## I want to send my little one to nursery, but some settings want them nappy-free before they start. I don't feel my daughter is ready for potty training. What shall I do?

If your little one is showing no signs that she is ready to be potty trained, I would recommend that you choose your childcare setting wisely. Potty training is not something that can be forced and starting too early can put huge pressure on both you and your little one. Your daughter is more likely to end up regressing if you try to train her before she is ready. I suggest that you choose a setting that doesn't require toddlers to be nappy-free.

## What should I do about daytime naps?

Most toddlers at potty training age still have a daytime nap. At the beginning of training, your toddler will not be quite ready to stay dry while they are sleeping and it can make them very distressed if they wake up with soiled pants so, for the first few weeks of potty training, ensure that your toddler sits on the potty/toilet before their nap and then use a nappy/pull-up for the duration of their nap, as you would for the night-time routine. Once your toddler has woken up with a dry nappy/pull-up over a period of a few weeks, you can leave their pants on for their daytime nap. Try not to make a big deal of putting the nappy/pull-up on – just say it is their 'special pants' for going to sleep. I never use the term 'nappy' after I have started potty training as I always tell my trainers that nappies are for babies and they are a big boy/girl now.

## Do we have to stay in the house while potty training?

From my years of experience with potty training it is a good idea to stay at home for the first two days. This will enable you to get the programme going and allow you to get into a routine, and give your little one time to grasp the concept in the comfort of their own home. As per my programme, I encourage you to get out of the house on Day Three. By this time you and your little one should be feeling confident enough and well into the potty training programme to have a short trip out. When you do venture out, please take your toddler's potty/trainer seat with you as it is important to keep the programme consistent and familiar for your little one while out of the home. Rewards have to be immediate to relate to what your toddler is doing at the time, so take some stickers/stars with you in case your toddler uses the potty/toilet. Once they return home they can put them on their chart or in their box. Do not venture too far and keep the journey short and close by. And don't forget the spare clothes and tissues! Don't leave it too long to venture out as we don't want your little one to associate potty training with just being inside the home.

## We have a holiday coming up and my toddler is showing signs of readiness. What should we do?

We all need to go on holiday and it is a lovely time to make special memories together as a family. If you have a holiday booked a few weeks down the line and your little one is showing signs they are ready for potty training then I would suggest you start before you go away. It is not a good idea to delay potty training for a few weeks when your toddler is indicating they are ready – you definitely do not want to miss this opportunity.

If you are in the early stages of potty training when you leave to go on holiday it is really important to keep the training on track and keep the continuity going for your toddler. Make sure you take your child's potty/

trainer seat and lots of spare pants and rewards with you. If you are going abroad, these can fit easily in your suitcase or, better still, carry them in your hand luggage to use at the airport or on the plane. Little ones tend to be very scared of airplane toilets – they are very noisy and, if I'm honest, I am not too keen on them myself, hoping I don't get sucked in ... what must it be like through a toddler's eyes?

Even if you feel you have cracked potty training when your holiday arrives, extra reminders will still be needed for your toddler. Remember, it is very exciting for them to be away and in different surroundings so they may forget to ask, which will lead to accidents. If you are going somewhere in the lovely sunshine, it is vital to make sure your toddler is properly hydrated – offer them extra fluid so they do not become dehydrated and to keep the bladder and bowel working as they should.

## What do we do if we're going on a car journey?

Try not to go on very long car journeys for the first couple of weeks, but if you have to, then stick with the programme but take regular breaks and encourage your little one to sit on the potty/toilet every time you stop. Lots of people ask whether they should put a nappy/pull-up back on their toddler for car journeys, but I think it's best to keep your child in big boy/girl pants as it can be very confusing and send mixed messages to toddlers if you revert to a nappy/pull-up. You need to avoid your toddler associating leaving the home with having to wear a nappy/pull-up.

Before you leave the house, make sure your little trainer sits on the potty/toilet for at least five minutes to avoid any accidents. A little trick of mine is to open up a spare nappy/pull-up and place it in the car seat, sitting the toddler on top, just in case of any accidents. This helps to protect the car seat and is more absorbent than a towel. It's a good idea to place the nappy/pull-up in the seat before your toddler gets in and preferably cover it over with a small blanket so they don't feel as though they have regressed. You can also use absorbent might mats or puppy trainer pads to protect the car seat – these are cheap to buy and will cover a larger area – but please make sure they do not obstruct the car seat fixings or seatbelt as safety comes first. Remember to be as discreet as possible if you decide to do this. Make sure you take spare clothes and pants with you and, if your toddler is using a potty/trainer seat, take this too as you don't want them to get caught short.

## What if my little one becomes poorly in the middle of potty training?

Some setbacks can be out of your control when you start potty training and toddlers do tend to pick up a lot of bugs. If your little one becomes sick and is really under the weather, is sleeping a lot and seems very lethargic, I would advise to temporarily stop potty training if you are only a week or so into it. Explain to your little one that you are letting them wear a nappy/pull-up again because they are poorly and, when they are better, they can have their big boy/girl pants back. If your toddler has been potty training for a couple of weeks and is showing good progress, I would see if you can work with it, keeping their big boy/girl pants on. However, if it becomes too much, then revert back to the nappy/pull-up and go back to pants when they are better.

## I have twins/triplets – how will potty training work?

Life would be just perfect if we could potty train our twins/triplets all in one go, but unfortunately this is not always the case. Each toddler will have their own rate of development and, just because they are twins/triplets, they will not necessarily be ready at the same time. If your little ones were also premature this could slightly delay potty training. I therefore recommend that parents treat their toddlers as individuals and, if one is showing signs of readiness but the other(s) is not, go with the one that is and the other(s) will normally follow in time.

I recommend that twins/triplets have their own individual reward system so they can be recognised for their individual achievements throughout the day. It is very important that toddlers feel special individually rather than sharing praise with their siblings. Separate reward systems will also help you when it comes to counting the rewards throughout the day and in the evening – it may be tricky for you to remember who achieved what if they share a chart. Believe me, I have potty trained many multiples and they have fantastic memories!

## My little boy has started to hide when he is doing a poo. I think this is due to a fear of pooing as he had a spell of constipation. What can I do?

Any child that has had constipation often holds on or refuses to tell you when they need a poo. This is because it would have hurt while passing the poo and now they have a fear. Your son will need a lot of reassurance and I would introduce a special reward system for when he does a poo. Make it very clear to him that poos have to come out so that he can eat some of his favourite foods and explain this to him in a simple way. Let him know that every time he asks for or does a poo he will get a special reward – this is not bribery but instead is letting him know that it is okay to do a poo and actually it is a fun thing to do.

## My little girl has been potty training for two weeks, but I still have to keep reminding her to go rather than her coming up and asking me. How can I change this?

This is a very common question. Most little ones will sit on the potty/toilet once Mummy/Daddy has reminded them, but what you need to start doing now is prompting your daughter rather than telling her to go. Try saying to her: 'If you need to go for a wee or poo ask Mummy/Daddy as you are a big girl now.' It's also really good to reward your daughter once she starts asking you to go to the potty/toilet as this will teach her that she has done something very special.

## What happens with potty training if my toddler attends a childcare setting?

If your toddler attends a childcare setting, I recommend that you have at least a few days together to start your potty training programme before they have to go to nursery. I cannot stress enough to always communicate your intentions with the setting and relay to them what you have been doing at home. Consistency is so important and most settings are happy to follow what you have been doing at home, so it is a good idea to buy extra pants that you can leave at nursery or pack in your toddler's bag as little ones do not like to be dressed in others' clothes. (Don't forget to name any pants or clothes you take in!)

I have worked with many childcare settings that are happy to continue my magic reward box/chart system as long as you put the stars/stickers in a clear bag with your child's name on. Your toddler's rewards can then be given throughout the day as you would at home, but make sure they are handed back to you to at the end of each day so your toddler can put the stars/stickers they have earned in their box or on their chart once they get home.

You may find your toddler is having repeat accidents while in their setting. This can be very common as there are lots of distractions and they may not be getting the one-to-one attention they are used to receiving at home. If this is the case, make an appointment with your child's key worker to discuss this as soon as possible so it does not undo everything you have achieved so far. Working with your child's childcare setting is key to their development.

## My little one will only use his own potty and when he is at nursery he is having lots of accidents. What can I do?

This suggests to me that you need to speak to your son's nursery and ask if your little one can take his own potty into nursery with him every day. It sounds to me that he has become very familiar and comfortable with his own potty. It is completely normal for toddlers to become attached to the potty they have been using, so just go with it. This doesn't have to be a long-term thing – it's just until your son grows in confidence and becomes fully toilet trained.

## My two-and-a-half-year-old son has told me he doesn't want to wear his night-time nappy anymore, but he wakes up wet every morning. Should I start waking him up to go on the potty?

Before you take the step of interfering with his and your good night's sleep, try getting your son into a bedtime potty routine. Reduce liquids at least 30 minutes before bedtime and make sure he sits on the potty/toilet for 5–10 minutes before he goes to bed. Do make sure he is drinking plenty of fluid throughout the day to ensure he isn't going to bed thirsty. You can try these steps to prepare him for night-time training but, as he is still waking up wet every morning, it indicates to me that he may not be fully ready yet. I would wait until he is showing the signs of readiness outlined on page 29.

# My son is 29 months old and showing signs that he is ready. He also tells me when he needs to go to the toilet but he refuses to use a potty or the big toilet. What should I do?

It is important to get your son involved and engaged in the discussions about using the potty/toilet. Pick a good potty training storybook, read it with him regularly and try to make it fun. Start asking him questions about the book to get him interested – this will give him a better understanding of what he has to do. Try using flashcards (see page 45) as this will help to get the message across using pictures rather than commands.

Give your son time to get used to the potty before he uses it by leaving it in the room where he spends most of his time and keep reminding him that it is there. Introduce a fun and exciting reward system which will encourage him even more.

Try to be patient and not too persistent as he may need just a little bit more time to grasp the concept.

# Conclusion **A Final Word for the Grown-Ups**

I hope that now you have reached the end of the book your potty training journey has been successful and you have felt that I have been with you every step of the way. I'm sure you have encountered all sorts of setbacks on this journey, but I hope you have found my programme and techniques fun and engaging and that they have helped this difficult milestone become more enjoyable for both you and your little one. Not only is this a big achievement for your toddler, but for you as a parent it's another great lesson you have taught your child.

If you have reached this point and your little one is still not quite fully potty trained please do not give up. You have done such an amazing job so far following my programme so keep going. Remember you will get there in the end – some little ones do take a little longer than others.

As you go through the years watching your children grow and develop you will come across different milestones – from schools and exams to boyfriends, girlfriends and teenage moods – but there is one thing we should all be grateful for and that is the miracle of a child. We have been blessed with them and they have got this far because of you. Being a parent is something we should all treasure. Enjoy every moment as this is an unconditional love like no other.

We learn every day, and sometimes parenting is challenging and frustrating. However, no matter what, you must remember that as long as you have tried your best to guide your child through life, that's all that matters.

I would like to take this opportunity to thank you for using my programme and to wish you the very best of luck with your onward journey and the next milestone that you and your little one will encounter.

Much love

Amanda

# Appendix

## Example Reward Chart

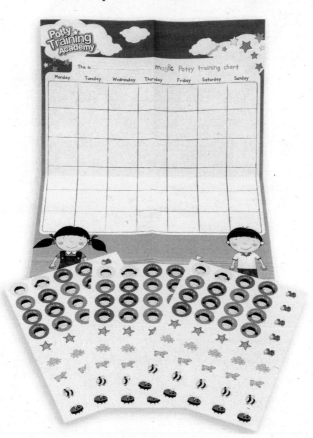

# Example Magic Reward Box

# Example Flashcards

wee in the potty

washing hands

good boy sitting on the toilet

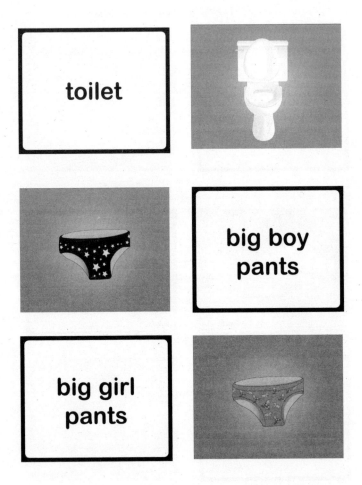

toilet

big boy
pants

big girl
pants

# Index